childless

Sian Prior is a Melbourne-based writer, broadcaster, musician and creative-writing teacher. She has been an ABC radio host and a regular columnist for the *Age/Sydney Morning Herald*. Her first book, *Shy: a memoir,* was published in 2014.

@sianprior

child less

a story of freedom and longing

sian prior

TEXT PUBLISHING MELBOURNE AUSTRALIA

The Text Publishing Company acknowledges the Traditional Owners of the country on which we work, the Wurundjeri people of the Kulin Nation, and pays respect to their Elders past and present.

textpublishing.com.au

The Text Publishing Company
Wurundjeri Country, Level 6, Royal Bank Chambers, 287 Collins Street, Melbourne Victoria 3000 Australia

Published by The Text Publishing Company, 2022

Cover design by Chong W.H.
Cover image by iStock
Page design by Rachel Aitken
Typeset by J&M Typesetting

Printed and bound in Australia by Griffin Press, part of Ovato, an accredited ISO/NZS 14001:2004 Environmental Management System printer.

ISBN: 9781922458568 (paperback)
ISBN: 9781922459862 (ebook)

A catalogue record for this book is available from the National Library of Australia.

This book is printed on paper certified against the Forest Stewardship Council® Standards. Griffin Press holds FSC chain-of-custody certification SGSHK-COC-005088. FSC promotes environmentally responsible, socially beneficial and economically viable management of the world's forests.

I would like to sing a song
to the loose, the wandering
and the unattached
Beth Spencer, 'Vagabondage'

Some names have been changed to protect the privacy of individuals referred to in this memoir.

reminiscence

IT'S EARLY IN 2003 and we're staying in a motel on the south coast of Queensland. Brown brick walls, shiny brown bedspread. A minibar humming at my feet: handy for storing hormone drugs. I'm sitting in front of a dressing-table mirror, vials lined up in front of me, easing the hypodermic out of its little cocoon. The orange casing clings to the needle: a lovers' embrace.

The man sitting on the bed behind me has his glasses on and he's reading a book. He's been silent for a long time. I look up from the paraphernalia on the dressing table and watch him in the mirror, watch his eyes scanning the page. Watch him not watching me, because this has nothing to do with him.

Then I pinch the skin of my belly between two fingers and slide the needle in.

inheritance

IT'S LATE SUMMER 2018. I've taken the afternoon off work and driven the campervan to the beach. I lie in the hot sun, reading a book set in Iceland. On page seventeen there is a sentence that makes me pause.

'On such a day the sun is stronger than the past.'

I close the book. Remind myself to breathe. Is this one of those days? The sun is right there, above me. I could look at it, but it would hurt, like the past.

On the way back the traffic is terrible. Peak hour—all those drivers heading home to their families. I pull up at the lights behind a little red car. In the lowering sun the backseat passenger is a shadow puppet, a dark blob swaying in the rear window. The figure in the back seat turns and becomes a profile: a long sharp nose, almost a beak. A bird-woman with the blurry jaw line of middle age. Her arms are reaching towards a child's car seat and her movements become jolly, that's the only way to describe it, a jolly kind of bouncing, as a tiny shadow arm pokes out from the car seat, reaching for the woman.

A third shape forms in the gloom, turning and peering backwards from the front passenger seat. The same long nose; the same jaw, but tauter. The child, the mother of the child, and the mother of the mother, three generations of beak-nosed shadow people together in the tiny red car, all looking jolly in the peak-hour traffic jam.

In my van, behind the tinted glass of the windscreen, I take one hand off the steering wheel and place it on my breastbone to hold the past where it hurts. I watch the light glinting off the rear window in front of me and try to remember just how strong the sun can be.

disappearance

IT'S SUMMER, LATE 2003. I'm back on the Queensland south coast, but this time I'm alone. Venturing out of my motel room for a swim, I've trudged around the end of the surf beach to a sheltered cove. There's a weathered jetty reaching out towards the horizon. Below, green algae dances around barnacled poles while the fishermen above wait patiently, squinting into the sun. I was planning to visit my father's beach today. It's close, just a couple of kilometres further south, but my courage has failed me again.

Halfway down the jetty I pause to peer into a bucket. The lone fish in the bottom has stopped flapping, but its gills are still gaping compulsively, waiting for some sweet salt water to fill them with life. Instead, another fish is thrown on top of it, and the leaping dance begins again.

I turn away from the jerking bucket towards the sunlit

end of the jetty. There are a few small boats bumping gently against the tyres tied to the wharf; hopeful seagulls strutting in circles around the fishermen. As I approach they lift off and hover till I pass, then resume their patrol.

Ahead of me a young blonde woman is pushing a flimsy stroller over the uneven planks. Her head is bowed, her bony shoulders hunched. She makes no attempt to navigate the gaps between the timbers, and the stroller lurches and swerves like a toy car. Hard to tell from behind whether it has a passenger. I slow my steps to create more distance between us.

When I finally reach the end of the jetty the young woman is sitting smoking with her legs dangling over the edge, her back to the land. There *was* a passenger after all, a girl of about four. She's standing behind her mother, poking her between those hunched shoulder blades. The child has Shirley Temple curls, thin legs and turned-in toes, which right now are scuffing rhythmically against a protruding nail.

There's a bench seat on the left side of the jetty's end, and I perch gingerly on it, trying to avoid the bird droppings. So good to sit down. It took me a long time to get to sleep last night and the five-thirty alarm crashed in on my dreams like a runaway train while Tom slept right through. Now the early-morning flight from Melbourne is catching up with me.

It's over. No more trips to the clinic. No more injecting myself with expensive vials of liquid fertility. Just the two of us from now on.

From behind my sunglasses, I pretend to be taking in the view while I watch the mother and daughter.

'Look at that bird, Mum, Mummy, Mum, Mum, look, look at that bird, Mum.'

The young woman looks, but in the opposite direction. She sucks hard on her cigarette.

'Mum, look, it's got a leg gone, Mum, look, Mum, where's its leg, look, where's it gone?'

The girl pokes at her mother's shoulder again. 'Mum, can you see it, where's it gone, Mum, I saw it, only one leg, Mum, did a shark eat it?'

The woman slowly turns her head and stares at the prodding child. 'Go. Away. NOW.' Her voice is tight and low, but loud enough for the nearby cluster of nervous seagulls to hear. They shuffle along the jetty, away from the angry human.

The girl gives up on her prodding and wanders towards the birds. Suddenly she's running at them, waving her hands. I lean forward, leg muscles tensed. Just before the girl reaches the edge of the jetty the squabbling gulls rise as one, circling back towards the shore. The child stops and stands with her hands flung wide as if to catch any tardy gulls. 'Gone,' she says, to the air in front of her.

Turning around, she notices me for the first time and comes trotting over. She clambers up onto the bench and shifts her bottom from side to side until she's braced against the back of the seat. Her thin legs are touching my thighs as she beams up at me.

'My name's Ashley, what's yours?'

'Sian.' I smile back at the blinking blue eyes. 'My name's Sian.'

The girl considers this information for a moment, her fingers scratching at the dried bird shit.

'Shine,' she says at last. 'Like the sun?' She's not interested in the answer. She's standing up now and leaning over the railing, staring into the broth of dark blue below us. 'I can see a lot of fish down there, can you see them, Shine? Look, I think they can see me, maybe they're scared of me, do you think they are?'

I want to put my hands around the girl's jiggling legs in case she pitches headfirst over the railing, but I hesitate. She is someone else's child. The girl's mother is fishing around in her cigarette pack, seemingly oblivious. My heart beats faster.

Ashley's feet have lifted off the ground now and she's hanging over the edge, balanced on her belly. I take hold of her ankles and tug them gently.

'Careful, Ashley, you might fall. Then the fish really *would* be scared. And I would be too, and your mum. Can you swim?'

She doesn't resist. Planting her feet firmly on the bench again she turns to me and places her hands on my head. 'Your hair's all wet, Shine, have you been swimming? Did you see a shark?' She moves her face close to mine, teeth bared, smiling a crazy shark smile. I glance over her shoulder towards her mother, who still hasn't turned around.

I could just take her. I could pick her up and run and run to the end of the jetty, before her mother notices. I'll hold her tight and when we get to the hotel I'll leave some cash beside the bed, close my suitcase and grab her hand and we'll run to the taxi rank and I'll tell the driver we're late for a flight to make him go fast, and we'll jump on the first plane back to Melbourne and we'll be up, up and away before her mother has even realised she's disappeared. And her mother might think she's fallen in the water and drowned, and she might just shrug her shoulders and abandon the stroller and go back to doing whatever she was doing with her young life before the baby came along. And we'll all live happily ever after—me, Tom and Ashley.

Or maybe just me and Ashley.

I breathe out. 'Ashley, I have to go. You should get back to your mum, she might be missing you.'

The woman is lying back on the wooden planks with her arms clasped behind her head, eyes closed, a new cigarette standing to attention between her lips.

'Bye-bye Shiney-shine.' Ashley slips off the seat. Dropping to her hands and knees she begins crawling across the splintery wood towards the prone woman. 'I'm a shark and I'm gonna eat my mum.'

Crossing my arms over my chest, I shove my hands into my armpits and walk back down the jetty towards the land. The sea breeze pushes me from behind, out of harm's way.

⌒

Did you read that news story about the baby who washed up on a Gold Coast beach? Nine months old. Her father

8

threw her into the harbour at Tweed Heads in the middle of the night. I want to hold that man's head under the water until he stops breathing, so he knows how she must have felt, sucking the sea into her lungs. Coughing, gulping. Rolling around in the wet dark, waiting for safe arms to grab her.

We're allowed to feel anger when it's clear who's at fault. We can be angry with the neglecters and the abusers and the murderers. It's expected. But anger is not acceptable in a situation like mine. Sorrow is okay but it should be quiet, modest sorrow. A head tilt, a tiny movement of the shoulders. *Oh well. Shit happens.* A stiff upper lip is good. Counting one's blessings, accepting the roll of the dice: highly commended. Not anger.

Not with the man whose children I miscarried. Not with the other man who didn't want to have a child with me. Not with the doctors who failed to diagnose the problem. Not with the people who jumped to conclusions about why I was not a mother. I'm not even allowed to be angry with my own body, not allowed to think of it as a failure. Just bad luck.

But the anger exists and it doesn't evaporate like spilt gin. It goes underground. It comes out in dreams. I'm shouting at all the men and all the doctors and all the ignorant people. I wake with a heaving chest and questions caught in my throat. *How did this happen? Whose fault is this?*

chance

LET ME TELL YOU a story that began not far from where Ashley became a shark.

I have never seen my father move. I've heard stories about him and seen black-and-white photos of a tall young trumpet player with my jawline. My existence is proof that he once existed. My love of making music probably comes from him. But somewhere deeper than my conscious mind, he has never quite seemed real.

Fifty-five years ago, on a beach near the border of New South Wales and Queensland, my father ran into the surf to rescue a pair of drowning swimmers. I was on the beach that day, a newborn baby wrapped in my mother's arms. So, yes, I *have* seen my father move, but no memories survive.

The story of what happened that day has two different endings, depending on when you press *pause*. The happy ending: my father swam out to the struggling swimmers and hauled them both back to the safety of a sandbank.

The unhappy ending is that after he rescued the swimmers my father disappeared under the waves. A week later he reappeared, a bloated corpse washed up on another beach. His body may have been attacked by a shark; the newspapers were divided on the subject.

When a man dies heroically, he can seem too good to be true. Perhaps that's why my father has always been like someone I've seen in a dream.

In 2018 a family friend sends me a photo of my father that I haven't seen before. In this photo he is playing the trumpet in a youth orchestra—and there is a huge old movie camera trained on him. If someone was filming him, could that footage still exist?

With the help of the National Film and Sound Archive of Australia I discover that a short documentary was made at a national music camp in 1955—the year the photo was taken. The archive people promise to send a copy of the film down to their Melbourne office for me and my sister Yoni to watch. Did our father make the final cut? I try to steel myself for disappointment.

A couple of weeks later Yoni and I meet up at the archive office. We're led into a small room and invited to sit in front of a computer screen. We hold hands; I press *play*. Five minutes in, I stop breathing.

On the screen a tall young trumpeter is sitting behind a music stand. He has big hands and a strong jaw, just like mine. He licks his lips. He blows a raspberry. He takes a deep breath, presses the mouthpiece to his chapped lips and blows.

I press *pause*.

My dream-father is real.

coincidence

IN THE BOOKS I READ as a child there were good guys and bad guys. There were those who deserved happy endings and those who didn't: a moral order.

I should probably have paid more attention to the games we played at childhood birthday parties. Musical chairs. Pass the parcel. Pin the tail on the donkey. It wasn't about who tried the hardest or who deserved to win. It was about where you were when the music stopped. Who had the parcel when it was time to tear off the last layer. Whether you were facing the donkey when you stopped spinning. It was random.

And the truth is, not all the stories had happy endings. Some had no ending at all. There were certain books in our house I couldn't bear to open. I knew exactly where they were—at the bottom of the bookshelf in the living room—and averted my eyes whenever I walked past them. One was a book on Australian wildlife containing detailed life-size illustrations of spiders. Redbacks, huntsmen, funnel-webs—I'd seen them once and that was enough. Another was a children's book with a picture on the front cover of a man chasing a black hat blown away by a strong wind. The hat had evil powers, the man was desperate, and I could feel the evil and the desperation from the other side of the living room.

There was a third book on the bottom shelf I couldn't look at. It had a picture inside the front cover of a giant wielding a cudgel. He had red hair and a red shirt and a gaping smile; he was striding through surf, where one huge foot had just sent two children tumbling headfirst out of a boat and into the pounding waves. On the shore two other children were running away from the grinning giant. The words on the page came from the mouth of the giant, who apparently spoke in rhyming couplets:

> Fee fi fo fum,
> I smell the blood of an Englishman:
> Be he alive or be he dead,
> I'll grind his bones to make my bread.

I still remember the yawning horror of the giant's grin and the sound those grinding English bones made in my imagination.

The things we fear usually catch up with us. Somehow that book has ended up in my possession. It's stained with age now, the spine peeling, the giant's red shirt fading to pink. There are some details in the picture that I'd forgotten. In the water behind the giant, a man is drowning. Another drowned man lies facedown on the beach.

I don't remember making the connection when I was a child. Now I find myself wondering—who thought this book was a good gift for children who'd lost their father to drowning? Who leafed through these pages and didn't see the pounding surf or the flailing man? Or maybe this book was in our family before our father disappeared under the waves. Maybe he read it to my sister at bedtime, not realising that The End—his end—was hidden in those pages.

On the back cover of the book there's a picture of a lion and a unicorn sitting up at a table, drinking tea. Someone has scribbled all over them with a violent black pencil. Perhaps it was me. Perhaps when I couldn't bear to look at the murderous giant I turned the book over and paid out on the happy couple.

patience

I ALWAYS ASSUMED it was a matter of when, not if, I would have a child. Growing up, I was the one in my family who the younger cousins gravitated towards. They knew I found them interesting, the questions they asked, the logical illogic of their brains. I liked the way they trusted me on the basis of very little information. Were my younger cousins like dolls for me? I was always the boss. I could teach them about the world from the great height of my few years' seniority. I could make the rules, change the rules, praise them for following the ever-changing rules.

I had dolls, too. There was one called Rosalind who'd lost a leg. Sometimes I tried to play with her but the missing limb made me teary. I would search for that plastic leg under my bed, under my brother's bed, in the bottom of the toy drawer, over and over. It must be somewhere. Things don't just disappear, surely? Then I'd abandon the search and Rosalind would end up back in the toy drawer. Until the next time.

There was another doll in that drawer whose long blonde hair grew longer when you pressed a button in her belly. Her hair was so magnificent, she had no need for a name. Or perhaps because she was so perfect, I couldn't love her enough to name her.

Back then, adults believed that young girls loved dolls because girls would eventually have babies. Dolls, they thought, were little plastic offspring for us to take care of, because girls were always and inevitably practising for motherhood. But for me, dolls were not so much pretend babies as diminutive adults, and I practised the rituals of adulthood with them—making the choices for them that would be available to me when I grew up. Choosing their clothes. Styling their hair. Controlling their socialising with other dolls. Moving them around a doll's house, through spaces where I imagined they had dominion. Babies had no dominion, not even over their bowel movements. Children had little more. I spent my childhood impatient to be an adult and dolls were my imaginary entrée into that world.

Sometimes my grandparents took me on holidays with the younger cousins, down to their fibro beach house on the surf coast. We made cubby houses out of fallen branches in the nearby forest. We ran races along the wet sand at low tide and jumped into the deepest rock pools and dog-paddled in circles with strands of seaweed draped over our scalps.

Our grandmother kept watch above us, applauding our magnificent slimy hair.

Sometimes we played hide and seek in the beach house, and I hid in places where my cousins wouldn't think to look, places it took an older, more strategic brain to find. Under a saggy beanbag. Behind the mouldy shower curtain. Then I waited, heart thumping, until their calling voices were about to tip from fun into fear, from hope into despair. *Find me/ don't find me*—I wanted both things at once.

Sometimes I let the searching cousin sit with that despair for longer than I should have. Had some older child inflicted the same mild torture on me, taught me about that tipping point of imminent loss? Or was I re-enacting a family drama that had played out on another coast a decade before? Just as the cousin was about to give up, I would jump out from my hiding place and make everything right with the world. I craved their relief, their gratitude, their embrace.

Why *do* children love hiding games? Hide and seek, sardines, peekaboo. They're all about being lost and found, unsafe then safe again.

My child played hide and seek with me for a long time: hiding, stretching out the waiting.

convergence

IT'S 1989 and I'm cycling slowly across a bridge spanning an eight-lane freeway on my way to save the planet. I've spent the last three years campaigning on ozone depletion and global warming for the Australian Conservation Foundation, trying to wrap my unmathematical brain around the delicate sciences of climatology and oceanography; trying to make those delicate sciences into powerful stories that will nudge people to action.

In the process I've learnt things I wish I didn't know about the workings of the circumpolar vortex and the potential loss of island nations. The world has become a different place, full of institutional roadblocks and oblivious over-consuming humans. At least one of my campaigning mates has given up on the idea of having children. When he turned thirty he had a vasectomy. 'Adding to the population will only make things worse,' he told me. 'Why create people you love and condemn them to an uncertain future on an overheating planet?' It was hard to argue against his logic.

But I still want a child. Not right now, I'm too young and too busy, but later, definitely. One would be great. A second would be a bonus. No more than that, because I don't want to make the overpopulation problem worse. And my child will try to save the planet, just like me.

Cycling against the wind, I turn my head and see long lines of vehicles stretching eastward to the outer suburbs of Melbourne. The cars are not moving. They're idling, waiting for the peak-hour crush to dissipate, spewing out carbon dioxide.

I brake to a standstill on the side of the bridge and stare at the ribbons of cars snaking out to the horizon, and it overtakes me at last, the dread I've been pushing down for the last three years. It rises from the pit of my gut to my throat and I hear myself: I'm whimpering. Standing astride a stationary bicycle above the freeway, fingers white-knuckled on the handlebars, I'm crying, because now I know.

I can't do it. The end of the world is nigh and it's my fault because I haven't done enough and can never do enough. I'm too small and too tired and too afraid of the future. I swivel the bike around, scrape away the tears and ride home again as fast as my legs can manage.

～

Three decades later a Swedish schoolgirl is addressing a United Nations climate summit in New York and she's snarling. She's lecturing the grown-ups about tipping points, feedback loops, climate justice, betrayal and forgiveness. She wants to cry, I can feel it in my own throat, but she won't. She's a genie released and she's trying to magic up some shame before it's too late.

I do the maths. She is exactly the age my first child would have been. And I'm one of the grown-ups she's lecturing.

adherence

IT IS 1992 and I'm having a fling. I've thought of my relationship with Jack as a fling for an unusually long time. The word has never felt quite right, though. Too carefree for someone like me; too much loose energy. A verb, not a noun. Still, it implies a get-out clause. Flings aren't meant to last.

Jack is a university lecturer and jazz musician, and he sings in the back row of the trade union choir, which I conduct. I've quit my job in the environment movement to run music programs out of Trades Hall. The looming climate catastrophe seems a long way away when we're singing 'Solidarity Forever' in two-part harmony on a dawn picket line.

For at least three hours a week Jack's eyes are on me. After rehearsals the choir crosses the road to the pub, where

Jack's eyes are still on me. I've been single for over a year and miss having someone looking at me. There is the matter of the age gap—I'm in my late twenties and Jack is in his early forties—but that's part of the reason I fancy him. It gives the fling a frisson. (Many romance-related words start with an F. *Fling. Fantasy. Father-figure.*)

Is our 'fling' a winning combination of naughty and safe? Jack's love is a steady, ever-ready thing. Those hands of his are always warm, always reaching for mine. They move over a piano keyboard like tandem skiers tackling moguls, leaping and sliding fearlessly across the black and white landscape. When Jack plays jazz, I know my heart is in safe hands.

About a year after Jack and I get together, one of the women in our choir announces she's pregnant. Catherine keeps coming to rehearsals right up until the week she gives birth. We all feel proprietorial about that new baby. A few weeks after her daughter is born Catherine brings her to visit, and I end the rehearsal early so we can spend some time admiring the product of Catherine's labour. The women jostle for a hold, offering up their fingers for the baby to grab. In the early nineties newborn babies are still considered women's business, and most of the men hold back.

Not Jack. He quizzes Catherine about the details of the birth, then asks if he can have a hold too. Catherine offers him the snuffling bundle without hesitation; Jack picks her up oh so gently with those warm hands of his. Cradling the baby in the crook of his arm, he smiles down at her. I'm watching his face, every nuance, wishing time would slow down so I won't miss a single muscle movement. Jack has tuned out the buzz of chatter and is entirely focused on the breathing mass of soft new flesh in his care. He looks like a father.

This. This is something important, this tenderness. The 'fling' is over. Something else has begun.

vigilance

IT'S 2016. I'm watching a group of kids playing on the grassy foreshore at Byron Bay, a bunch of them rushing down a steep concrete slope onto the beach. One small blond boy—maybe four years old, maybe younger—stops at the top. He considers the ramp for a long time. Finally, stepping gingerly in loose gumboots, he walks down the slope onto the beach. Then he turns and climbs back up again. Ignoring the calls of the other children, he trots across the grass towards the top of a rock wall.

Jagged grey boulders are lodged unevenly against the edge of the foreshore park, a barrier against the ever-rising tides. The boy takes off his floppy gumboots and places them carefully where they won't fall. Then he climbs slowly down, barefoot, over the boulders. I want to applaud him. *Bravo!*

There is a mother there, watching and waiting as her son

negotiates the treacherous rocks. Patience and trust. Is that what it takes to be a good parent? *Bravissima.*

The next day, same beach. Another small boy, playing with his father. From a distance they look picture-perfect, the son digging a hole in the wet sand, the father crouching in front of him, staring intently at the activity. Closer up it looks different. The father is not watching his son shovelling sand. He's staring down at his phone, reading and tapping and swiping.

As I near them the father is shouting at the boy. 'No, no, don't, just don't, why on earth, no, don't…You idiot!' He's shaking his phone, which must have copped some of the wet sand. The man turns and stomps towards the boy's mother, waving the phone under her nose and gesturing back towards the scene of the crime. *Dobber.*

As I pass them the mother is shouting at the boy. 'You've been very, very bad, you hear me? Why are you so bad? What do you mean you don't care?'

Don't judge, Sian. You haven't been there. The wind blows most of her words away, but still, some linger. *So bad. Don't care.*

—

In another book from my childhood there was a picture of a hairy giant with many mouths holding a tiny naked baby upside down by her feet. The baby was called Cuddlepie, I wasn't fooled by the cute name. This was not a cuddly The hairy giant—who was called a Wicked Banksia

26

Man—was dangling the baby over a deep hole. Did he let go of her? I can't remember. The book was banished to the bottom shelf, along with the one containing the red-headed giant in the surf.

When I was a child my grandmother Peg used to sing me this lullaby—

> Rockabye baby in the treetops,
> when the wind blows the cradle will rock,
> when the bough breaks the cradle will fall,
> down will come baby, cradle and all.

Back then I loved it, but now it sounds like a nightmare. There are other scary lullabies. There's a Spanish one about a wolf coming to eat the child, and a Brazilian one where it's not a wolf but an ox. In Haiti it's a crab, and in Italy it's a wicked old hag. There's always something terrible coming to take the child away—but an old woman?

I don't think the wicked old woman had children of her own. That's what made her a hag.

confidence

IT IS 1997 and Jack and I have been together for five years. I've finally packed up all my books and moved into his place. Every morning at the same time he brings me a cup of tea in bed—Jack loves routines—and every morning I'm grateful for his kindness. And his optimism. Whenever the world seems too bleak to bear, I can rely on Jack to talk me around. In his world view, goodness outweighs evil. We just need the right systems in place to enable that goodness.

'The thing is, Sian,' he says, 'we have to keep fighting the good fight until we win.' It always strikes me as an odd metaphor for such a peaceable man, but Jack has the sturdiest moral compass I've ever encountered. I envy his certainty about right and wrong.

We're a two-piano household now and he spends hours noodling on the keyboard in his study. Jack's diligence encourages me to park myself beside the other piano and do my singing practice more regularly. My career path has taken another swerve and for the past couple of years I've been working as a radio journalist at the ABC. Although no longer a paid environmental advocate, I've been elected to the ACF Council and am still involved on the periphery of campaigns. It helps with the guilt. And Jack and I have decided to have a baby. I'm thirty-three, he's forty-seven. It's time.

I've always thought my early thirties would be the ideal age to have children. A boy and a girl would be great, a couple of years apart would be ideal. It's an excellent plan, particularly since I'm now working for an institution that offers maternity leave. So, it's decided.

A month after going off the pill I realise my period is late. I pee on the little white stick and bingo—two blue lines. Easy as that.

Jack and I are practical people. We buy a fat book called *What To Expect When You're Expecting* and study up on how to do pregnancy. On the author's advice we choose a maternity hospital and organise to go on one of their regular tours. Jack and I leave our offices early that day and meet up in the hospital foyer. We join a small group of pregnant women who are following a brisk nurse around the maternity ward. There are neatly made beds for the mums and orange bucket chairs for the dads and vases of flowers everywhere. Picturing myself hunkered down behind one of these blue cubicle curtains, I feel a trickle of fear.

At one point in the tour the nurse asks me how many weeks 'gone' I am. 'Seven,' I answer. Her eyebrows shoot up. 'Gosh. You've come in early! I'm not sure we've ever had anyone do the tour at seven weeks before.'

My face is suddenly hot. Perhaps we should have waited a bit longer before jumping into the logistics. When the tour ends Jack and I are the first to leave, hurrying into the lift together. Looking down I discover that a couple of my shirt buttons have come undone, exposing me. I'm blushing again, imagining the nurse shaking her head at my dishevelment. Why didn't Jack tell me about the buttons? I can't wait to get back to work, where I know what I'm doing.

A few days later I begin to bleed. We consult the pregnancy book. Spotting in the early stages of pregnancies is not uncommon—but these are not spots. More like the heaviest period I've ever had. The book calls it a 'spontaneous abortion'. I'm aware of the irony. I've always been a strong supporter of women's right to choose, and yet there's no choice involved in this one, it's just happening to me.

It's never crossed my mind that a pregnancy of mine could end like this. Maybe this has been a false start, preparing me for the real thing.

Next time I'll be ready.

innocence

IT'S 2018 and a scientist on the radio is saying that sharks like jazz. Apparently if you play them jazz, the sharks will come for the tasty morsels the scientists have prepared for them. 'Sharks have really big brains,' the scientist says, 'and are obviously much smarter than we give them credit for.' The scientist is hoping the sharks' jazz training will shift public and political will towards their conservation. The more an animal behaves like us, the more we think it has a right to live.

A decade and a half ago I played a jazz album to my three-year-old nephew. When Louis Jordan sang 'Jack, You're Dead', my nephew lay down on the floor. He put his head right up against the speaker and listened with his whole body. When the song ended, he asked me to play it again. And again, and again. A few years later my nephew started learning guitar. He quickly mastered the instrument, probably because he spent every spare minute of his life playing music. Next the piano. Then the drums.

Now my nephew is eighteen and he's in a bunch of different bands. He's invited me to a guitar gig he's doing in a bar. He's due to fly out of the country soon for his first big solo travel adventure. The set begins with a jazz tune. As I listen to the melody noodling out from under his fingers, I think about that little boy with his ear pressed to the speaker. I think about all the new music he'll hear on his travels. The trains he'll catch or miss. The strangers he'll befriend or avoid. The foreign languages he'll be immersed in or befuddled by. The wonderful terrible freedom he'll embrace, and the terrible wonderful homesickness that will embrace him. I think about the years and decades ahead of him, the rising temperatures, the disappearing coastlines. As the first tune comes to an end I clap and whistle louder than necessary.

The second song is one he's written himself. In the chorus he sings: 'And then, piece by piece, everything pushes you into unease'.

Suddenly I want to warn him to be careful. Tell him not to go near the sea if he's playing jazz. Warn him about what's coming down the line for him, as nature buckles under the weight of my generation.

endurance

IT'S 1999, more than a year and a half since the miscarriage. Eighteen menstrual cycles, frustratingly uninterrupted. With each failure to conceive, sex has felt more and more—for me at least—like a duty rather than a pleasure. The routine of trying at the 'right time of the month' weighs on me like a musty blanket. Has Jack been feeling the same way? We haven't been able to talk about it.

But now, at last, I am pregnant again. Seven weeks in (how quickly life has become about attaching numbers to weeks), my breasts ache. Waves of dizziness occasionally wash over me when I stand up too quickly or go too long without eating. I'm tired all the time, but I was already feeling like that before I conceived.

I'm presenting a weekly radio arts program for the ABC and there's a live broadcast planned at Heide, the museum of modern art. We'll set ourselves up in the gardens there, a pop-up studio with microphones on a trestle table. The producer and I have lined up a bunch of guests for me to interview over the three-hour program. Jack has decided to come along and be part of the audience.

The forecast is for a hot day. I slather sunscreen on my arms, fill my water bottle and drive us out along the freeway to the museum. As we pull into the carpark I feel the knot of tension in my gut tighten. *Showtime. Get your smile on, girl.*

The first hour goes smoothly, guests appearing on time, conversations flowing easily. Curators, musicians, writers and artists come and go from the long table, fumbling with their headphones and flirting with the crowd. Then, during the five-minute news break, I notice a pain in my belly. No, lower down. Could be nerves again…but it's a different kind of ache. Different, but familiar.

The second hour is harder. A side section of my brain is working very hard not to think about that ache. I interview an elderly French artist and she's so excited about having a live audience, she stands up from the table and does a series of tumbles on the soft grass. She's wearing flouncy cream knickerbockers and wants us to see them. The crowd whoops and whistles as she hauls herself up off the ground and falls back into her seat. Such freedom. I could never do that, couldn't not care about the exposure.

In the news break at the end of the second hour I skirt around the crowd and hurry across the grass to the women's toilets. Look down and freeze: blood everywhere. Thick dark clots of it. No time to deal with this. Two minutes till the mikes open. *Don't think about it. Keep moving.* The blood has leaked into the crotch of my trousers and only my habit of wearing too much black has saved me from the humiliation every girl knows—the hot shame of being a public bleeder.

I dab frantically and stuff wads of toilet paper into my undies, trying to calculate how much more blood there will be by the end of the show. *Thirty seconds till the news ends. GO.*

Later I will let myself feel what that blood means. Right now, I am gracious: a smiling hostess, chatting and nodding and laughing, my mind floating like a balloon above the table, ignoring the blood pooling between my thighs. Keeping the show going, counting the minutes till I can stop.

In that long hour I come to understand how they do it, people like the firefighters who protect other people's homes while their own are under threat. How they must lock up certain rooms in their minds and pocket the keys, so they can get the job done. *Not now. Later.* In between interviews I steal glances at Jack, sitting out there in the audience, grinning encouragement at me. Jack, who doesn't know yet. Jack, who still thinks we're parents-to-be.

At last, the theme music plays and I can sign off. A handful of keen radio listeners hover near the table, wanting to chat, but I keep my head down, gathering up pieces of paper, trying not to move too quickly in case the blood moves too. *Home. I need to go home.* The pain is knife-sharp now.

Jack approaches the table with a broad smile. Before he can say anything I mutter, 'We have to go. Now.' I stumble towards the carpark. Jack catches up and puts a gentle hand on my arm.

'The show was great, Sian. Everything okay?'

'No. I'll tell you in a moment.' I shake off his hand. I don't need gentle, I need to escape.

'Can you drive?' I hand him the keys and at last we're pulling out of the carpark and onto the road home.

'What's happened?' he asks.

'I'm—there's—I think—'

How *do* people say this? *I? We?*

'I think I'm having another miscarriage.' I can't look at him. My throat has begun to close up, and there's heat behind my eyes. *Not now. Not yet.*

'Oh,' he says quietly. 'You poor—'

'Don't,' I interrupt him. 'Not pity. I need you to distract me. Can you tell me a joke?' I stare straight ahead at the car in front of us, waiting. But Jack is silent.

The tears begin then, and they are tears of anger. Jack is the closest target. I've been entertaining *him* for the last three hours. Can't he tell me one lousy joke?

We don't go straight home that afternoon. We go first to the hospital: they arrange an ultrasound. I lie there in the middle of all the gleaming technology, midriff exposed. Jack holds my hand. The technician has her eyes fixed on a screen. Round and round she goes, backwards and forwards, then finally she speaks.

'There's nothing there. Nothing at all. Are you sure you were pregnant?'

I can't speak. Jack's grip tightens on my hand. 'Yes, of course,' he says.

'Well, it's gone. Nothing left.'

—

Two decades later I'm reading a newspaper article by a female TV host who achieved notoriety a few years ago when she made fun of an MP on national television. Not realising the camera was on her, she made a derisive gesture, and her moment of mockery was picked up and replayed hundreds of times. Her gaffe had baffled me. She was someone I'd always admired. She won a journalism award for calling out a lying politician; she always seemed so enviably in control on air. Now I understand. The day before the famous moment, the presenter had been given some wonderful news. After months of failed IVF treatment, and now in her mid-forties, she was finally pregnant. The morning of the big gaffe she was 'over the moon', she said now: her professional mask had slipped.

The morning of my on-air miscarriage I'd kept the mask firmly in place—but *why*? Why hadn't I told my producer what was happening and gone straight to a hospital?

There's a postcard stuck to my fridge with a drawing by one of my favourite cartoonists. On the postcard a woman is sitting in front of a radio microphone with a man leaning over her, and the man is saying, *If you could just try to sound less like a woman.* I like it because it's so familiar. During my radio career I was told many times to try to lower the pitch of my speech. 'Listeners don't like women's high voices,' I was told. I still hear them, the female sports broadcasters, the female current affairs hosts, all camped resolutely in the lower end of their vocal range, each trying to sound less like a woman. Even today, young women twenty or thirty years younger than me seem to need to prove that our high-pitched voices, our hormonally suspect, bleeding (or bulging) bodies are not professional liabilities. There's still an unspoken understanding that if we want to perform in previously male-dominated professions, we must pretend not to be female.

indifference

IT'S 2018 and I've driven the campervan up the highway from Melbourne to Mildura to run some writing workshops. There's a magazine called *Your Sunraysia* sitting on the coffee table in my rented unit. 'Making Dreams a Beautiful Reality', the headline says. A pink-cheeked baby with a pink crocheted headband and a pink floral dress smiling at the camera. Clear, wide-set blue eyes, a lick of blonde hair. She could have been mine. (Though I would never have decked her out in that girly-girl livery; more likely T-shirts featuring cute endangered critters. Same inclination to use a child as a billboard for my world view...)

The article is all about the success of the local IVF clinic. The language is familiar. Simpering. Infantilising. Nouns are diminutive; emotions are hesitant. In a 'little building' there's a 'small team' of specialists. The couples they see are 'suffering' infertility. They haven't had 'any luck'. But the doctors are 'there for them', 'walking the journey' with the luckless suffering couples. All that suffering is relieved when the women 'fall' pregnant and the couples are 'blessed' with a baby, sometimes two. The 'mums and dads' bring their pink-faced babies back to the little building for 'cuddles' with the 'IVF family' whose benign alchemy helped them to transform 'hopes into dreams'. The word 'cuddles' is used no less than five times in the article.

I once heard a linguist talking on the radio about something she called 'verbal cuddling strategies'. She was referring to the rituals we use when we're trying to seem friendly, cooperative, non-threatening in our communication. Words and phrases designed to avoid offending: *You know what I mean? Don't you reckon? If you don't mind?* Women are more likely than men to use this language, the linguist said, to avoid appearing 'overly assertive'. Could the word *cuddles* be part of a textual cuddling strategy? And if so, who is being textually cuddled—who is the imagined reader? Certainly not someone like me, someone reluctantly inducted into this world of 'fertility enhancement', someone who found it anything but cuddly.

I can't finish the article. Instead, I skim the photos—the container of frozen embryos that looks like a domestic rice cooker; the friendly scientists wearing blue hair nets and peering into microscopes; the obstetrician leaning on her desk, offering up a reassuring smile. They're all women. The journalist is also a woman. All the parents she interviews are women. It's a long time since I was a member of this baby-making club, more than a decade and a half. Looks like some things have changed.

~

It's early 2000. The waiting room of the IVF clinic is full of pregnant women. They're slotting coins into the vending machine, leaning back on couches, sipping takeaway coffees, strolling past us to the toilets, chatting with the receptionists. Their bulging bellies should be comforting— proof that the technology works. Somehow, though, their success makes it even harder to be sitting here, feeling like a naughty student outside the principal's office. How has it come to this?

I'm not a person who fails. That's not a boast, it's a neurosis. I've made sure that, from the outside, I look like a winner. A conscientious student. A hard-working employee. Life presenting as a series of exams; me making sure I pass them. On the rare occasions when I've failed in public I have been mortified beyond belief. The forgotten piano music at the school concert. The fall from the stage at a choir rehearsal. (I got straight back up and told everyone I was fine even though the bruise lasted months and the dent in my thigh lasted years.) If there is a high risk of failing at something, I give it a wide berth.

It simply never crossed my mind that I might fail at having children. That getting pregnant and staying pregnant were fail-able activities. Yet here we are, on a couch in a waiting room in a hospital clinic full of winners and losers.

Jack's hand reaches for mine. There's a slight tremor in his fingers and at this moment it feels like an extension of my racing heart. What will I say to the fertility specialist? We've both had a few tests done. There's a small scar below my navel, a permanent reminder of the laparoscopy that came up blank. There is a slightly lower than average sperm count. That's how I would put it—'there is', not 'Jack has'—otherwise it might sound like one of us is to blame.

We arrived early for the appointment and the doctor is running late. *Why are they always late?* The glossy magazines on the table in front of us look untouched. Do they bring fresh ones every day? Or is everyone here too nervous to read? Beside the magazines a vase of pink Asian lilies perfumes the pastel waiting room, making my eyes and nose itch. Pink again—the least offensive colour. A decor-based cuddling strategy? At last my name is called and we're shown into an office. A short man with a bow tie greets us, shaking hands firmly with Jack and gesturing towards two chairs. There are framed photos of children on the wall. I assume they're his, but perhaps they're some of the ones he's helped to create. Once we're all seated, I take the lead, explaining our history—the easy first pregnancy, the early miscarriage, the long wait for the next pregnancy, the second miscarriage, and the months and months of nothing since then.

'We're not ready to do full-on IVF yet, but we thought we should start exploring our options,' I conclude. The doctor nods, glancing down at a folder on his desk, then looks expectantly at Jack. 'We're very keen to have a family,' Jack says.

There they are again, those words. Jack knows how I feel about this phrase. *We ARE a family,* I want to say. *The two of us. It's not a family we want, it's a child.* Language can have the same kind of effect on me as those lilies—like an allergic reaction in my synapses—but Jack doesn't understand my vehemence. Neither do I, at this moment. Something about us, together, being enough.

The doctor begins talking. He draws diagrams on a notepad and lists the medications he can prescribe for me to 'enhance' my fertility. All the time he keeps his gaze fixed on Jack. After a while it's hard to listen because I'm so distracted by waiting for him to look at me. I'm the one who will be taking the drugs, not Jack. I'm the one whose egg production can be stimulated by the artificial hormones, to increase our chances of conceiving. I'm the one who will have to deal with the side effects the doctor mentions almost as an afterthought. I'm the one who will fall pregnant, as they say, if he can just push my recalcitrant body in the right direction. Or who will fail to fall.

After about fifteen minutes of this my brain simply gives up. There is no room for new information because there is too much rage in there. My face and torso feel hot with it. (Is this why I can't get pregnant? What sensible foetus would want to check in to this angry body?) Then the doctor is ushering us out, telling us his secretary will coordinate the appointments to organise more tests. He shakes Jack's hand once more and points us towards reception. As soon as the door closes behind him, I turn to Jack. 'No—not him,' I hiss. 'Let's get out of here.'

—

Two decades later I'm in my rental unit in Mildura, watching the evening news. There's a story about a man who has been passing himself off as a gynaecologist and fertility specialist. For a decade he had a Melbourne 'practice' where he gave injections and did 'internal examinations' on his 'patients'. His qualifications were forgeries, his earnings were in the hundreds of thousands of dollars. He promised one woman she would be 'pregnant by Christmas'.

'He preyed on women desperate for children,' the newsreader says. *Desperate.* They often use that word to describe us. There's no dignity in desperation. It's pitiful. Desperation leads to credulity. I was never desperate—this is what I've told myself over the years. I would never have fallen for this act. All a man had to do was avoid looking me in the eye and I lost faith in his magical powers.

Jack and I found another specialist, a woman. There were no photos in her consulting room, and no framed university degrees. There were abstract paintings and small sculptures, interesting objects without stories. It was a neutral space in which she explained to us how to 'increase our chances'. The terrible statistics and the role of dumb luck were both acknowledged. She didn't hide the fact that many people like us fail to get what they want, but she looked me in the eye and explained exactly how she could try to help us not fail again. We put ourselves in her hands.

transcendence

IT'S 2017 and I'm snorkelling off Lady Elliot Island, a coral cay at the southern tip of the Great Barrier Reef. Below me are handbag-sized clams with luminescent green lips and black sea slugs frosted with sugary sand. Every imaginable dance move is going on around me—flicking, swaying, shimmying, darting—a hyperactive ballet troupe, except the dancers are fish. This reef has all the art forms covered—the Rembrandt-blue starfish, the Ballets Russes damselfish, the Stravinskyesque percussion of a million tiny mouths nibbling on coral. Even football gets a look in. I nickname a little black and white guy the Collingwoodfish. Later I will discover there is another one called the Chinese footballer cod. We love to make other species seem human. Maybe we think they want to be just like us.

I've left the campervan on the mainland, at Hervey Bay,

and flown here in a light plane with about a dozen other daytrippers. The island is small: there's plenty of time to walk the circumference before lunch. The beach is strewn with the skeletal remains of staghorn coral, and as I skirt the shoreline, I have to work hard to resist pocketing some of the prettiest pieces. How can a graveyard feel like heaven?

Arriving back at my starting point on the beach I watch a woman trying to cajole her young son into going snorkelling. He's shaking his head and whimpering. There's scratchy sand in his fins. 'Don't you understand,' I want to whisper to him, 'this could be your last chance?'

After lunch our tour group trudges back to the beach to meet up with the cheery ranger who greeted us at the tiny airport this morning. A glass-bottomed boat is anchored in the shallows, but before we can board, the ranger has some less cheery information to impart. Mass bleaching has affected two thirds of the Great Barrier Reef in the last couple of years, he tells us, killing huge quantities of coral. The southern part of the reef, including Lady Elliot Island, sustained a bit less damage than the north. But there was worrying bleaching here last summer, halted only by the cooler currents that came with Cyclone Debbie. Some of the other tourists look as uncomfortable as I feel, but others tune out and stare at the horizon, impatient to get out there on the glinting water.

At last we're bobbing above the coral, preparing ourselves to slide overboard. The boy who wouldn't go snorkelling is leaning over the glass, spotting the fish and turtles mooching below us. With some gentle encouragement from the ranger he pulls his goggles on and eases himself into the water. As I kick away from the boat I catch sight of him churning like a paddle-steamer ahead of me, fins throwing up frantic bubbles as he chases something always just out of reach. I'm happy to float with the tide, watching shy clownfish peeking out from behind swaying anemone.

Half an hour later the boy hauls himself back onto the boat, teeth chattering, eyes wide with the shock of pleasure. 'I saw a manta ray!' he tells us. 'And Nemo!'

As I watch the boy's beaming mother towel him dry, I'm trying to find a word that captures the complex ecosystem of emotions I'm registering right now. The envy. The regret. The tamping-down of envy and regret. The curiosity. The painful pleasure of seeing another woman enjoying the thing I wanted so badly.

And I want to tell this child about the new word that's been invented to describe how you feel when something in the natural world is being destroyed before your very eyes. It's called *solastalgia*. I want to utter this sibilant word out loud and apologise to the boy for what's happening. For what we're allowing to happen. I don't, of course.

Later that afternoon, as we fly back to the mainland over the endless blue, there are whales to the left of us, dolphins to the right. Here we are, right in the middle of paradise, and we're running out of time.

⁓

A year later I receive an email from Change.org, a group that organises online petitions. More than eight thousand people, they tell me, have signed a petition to 'make the Great Barrier Reef a citizen' to 'ensure the protection of this natural wonder'. They want me to join them in supporting 'the reef's right to life'. I sign up immediately. Then I wish I hadn't. Nature shouldn't have to be more like us to be valued.

impatience

IT'S JULY 2018 and there are a dozen boys stuck in a flooding cave in Thailand. The whole world is watching the rescue effort. I can hardly bear to look away from the television. While I wait for someone to save them, I'm thinking about metaphors. Wet cavities with children stuck inside. Eggs hiding in the warm crevices of my reproductive system. Fragile embryos attaching themselves to slimy walls. The violent rush of liquid that is threatening to flush them out. The waiting. All the terrible hoping and waiting.

⁓

It's early 2001 and I'm hunched behind a blue curtain in an emergency-department cubicle in the Royal Women's Hospital, waiting for someone to come and stick another needle in my arm. Another vial of blood to be tested, another three-hour wait, the same response from the nurse—come back again in two days. Results: inconclusive.

It's been forty months since Jack and I first started trying to have a child. All we've managed are two early miscarriages. I've tried acupuncture, Chinese herbs, naturopathy, homeopathy, yoga, a caffeine- and alcohol-free diet, and fertility-boosting drugs prescribed by the IVF specialist. Nothing has worked. By the end of the year I'll be thirty-seven. Time is running out.

Jack and I have been waiting for my period, waiting for the absence of my period, waiting to have sex at the right moment, waiting for test results, waiting to feel less testy with each other. I've also been waiting to see if there is another job for me in radio. After presenting my own program for two years, my contract hasn't been renewed. I will not be back on air any time soon. I've accepted a redundancy package and headed home to wait for a new career path to emerge from the fog. I need time out. Get away from my old life. Escape the humiliation of having failed and failed again.

We know it's time to try IVF. We've even had dinner with a couple, friends of Jack's, who've been through it all. Ten years, it took them. Now they have two small children—they careened around the living room as we ate our meal. *Hardest thing we've ever done,* the husband said. *Nearly broke the marriage,* his wife added. As I watched them trying to persuade their kids to go to bed, I thought about broken things. About the ways failure and disappointment can bear down upon the fragile connections between bodies, fraying the bonds of desire. I thought about how I've begun to divorce my mind from my body during sex, so I won't feel how high the stakes are. About how my body is missing my mind, because that's where desire begins. Would IVF reverse this process for me—remove the baby-making enterprise from the arena of desire? Can our bodies find their way back to each other?

Before starting on the IVF program Jack and I will treat ourselves. Blow the redundancy package. Our first overseas trip since we got together nine years ago. We'll spend the end of the European spring in Italy and France, and the beginning of summer in Berlin, Prague and Istanbul. We need to do something together that's about pleasure rather than about waiting. Our flights are booked, and we've started packing our bags.

A week before we're due to fly out my period is late. There's one little white stick left in the bathroom cupboard. I peel off the packaging and pee on it. Two blue lines!

Shock. Elation. Panic. What if I miscarry again? It's bad enough when you're minutes away from one of the best maternity hospitals in this English-speaking country. How much worse would it be, stuck on a sleeper train to Prague? When Jack arrives home that evening and I give him the news, the same three emotions cross his face within the space of a few seconds.

We're both practical people. We shut down our feelings and make contingency plans. We have travel insurance; we can postpone our flights if necessary or change our itinerary.

We can't bear the idea of cancelling the trip. Jack needs a break, exhausted from long hours at work, and maybe from dealing with my misery. For me the stakes are even higher. One of the symptoms of my misery is a teeth-grinding irritability. The smallest thing can set me off. Waiting for Jack to finish shaving so I can use our tiny bathroom. Waiting for him to get home so I can dish up dinner. Waiting for him to finish reading the weekend papers so I can have a look. His steadiness—one of the things I've always loved about him—has lost its appeal. I'm not sure how much more waiting I can take.

Three days before we're due to fly out, I start bleeding. The bleeding is soon followed by sharp pain. *Here we go again,* I tell myself. *Better now than later.* I have my first glass of wine in a month. Then the bleeding stops. What the hell is going on? I buy another home pregnancy test. It's still coming up positive. Is this good news or bad? Why did I drink that wine? Poring over the dust-covered pregnancy book we bought years ago, before the first miscarriage, I find a chilling paragraph:

'Ectopic pregnancy: Brown spotting or light bleeding, intermittent or persistent, accompanied by abdominal and/or shoulder pain, which can often be quite severe.'

The embryo implants in a fallopian tube instead of the uterus and is without exception 'non-viable'.

We head to the hospital. A blood test to check hormone levels. An ultrasound. The doctor is optimistic. There's a tiny blip on the screen. She thinks the pregnancy is in the uterus, and still viable. I need to have more blood tests over the next week, to make sure things are progressing normally. It'll be a hassle, finding hospitals in foreign countries, but we're practical people. We'll manage. Anything rather than cancel the trip.

Later that day we return to the hospital for the blood-test results. A different doctor is on duty and she's less confident. Yes, I *am* pregnant, but there's a high risk of it being ectopic. She doesn't think I should fly. If the fallopian tube ruptures during an ectopic pregnancy it can kill you. She tells us to come back in forty-eight hours for another blood test.

We drive home in silence, sick with fear and disappointment. Jack makes frantic calls to the airline and the travel insurance company to put our flights on hold indefinitely. We spend the next couple of days weeding the garden, both of us ricocheting between hope and frustration. Back to the hospital—another ultrasound. It gets worse. They can see nothing in my uterus but there *is* something in one of the tubes. They might have to operate. 'Operating' on a fallopian tube is usually code for taking it out, which would halve our chances of conceiving naturally. It'll take weeks for me to recover. Our holiday will have to be cancelled.

Yet again, another hospital doctor has a different opinion. It might *not* be ectopic, he says. We should go away for another forty-eight hours, then check the hormone levels. If they don't fall rapidly, it probably *is* ectopic and still growing. They can give me a small dose of chemotherapy to kill off the remaining cells. At best, the drugs will make me feel crook. At worst, my hair will fall out.

The next day I wake with severe pain and spend the morning back in the emergency dept. A large clot of something—I can't bear to look too closely at it—dislodges itself from my insides. Once again the doctors send us home: 'Come back in another forty-eight hours.' This becomes the pattern for the next two weeks. Every couple of days I'm tested to see whether the hormone levels have gone down. Until they level out we won't know what's happened. I still might need an operation or a dose of chemo at the end of it all. Meanwhile, it's summer in Europe and we're not there. I borrow every foreign-language film in the local video store and use up all my hankies, crying over...What? A lost holiday? A lost child? The possibility of a lost fallopian tube, and a normal pregnancy?

After a fortnight, the hormone levels drop far enough that it's safe for me to leave. The final diagnosis is still unclear; it's possible there's been permanent tubal damage. But we can still get to Europe before their winter sets in. Perhaps the pleasures of travel will distract me. But will they stop my recurring dreams about trying to save small children from danger?

⁓

Fee fi fo fum, thunders the red-headed giant as he strides through the waves—*I smell blood.*

abundance

IT'S THE MIDDLE OF 2001 and I've been to the opera in Prague wearing purple leopard-print pyjamas, drunk myself stupid on blonde beers in Berlin and eaten so many four-course meals in France that I can no longer fit into most of my clothes—hence the opera pyjamas. I'm doing all the things I would never have done back home, but I am still me. Still childless.

In Berlin, Jack and I meet up with Kris, an old friend of mine from the environment movement. He's on leave and keen to do more travelling, so we morph from a pair to a trio. It's good to have someone new to talk to—after weeks of being together twenty-four seven, Jack and I are running out of things to say to each other. Kris has many friends in Europe and he organises a couple of weeks' accommodation for us in a beach house in Sardinia. It belongs to his German ex-girlfriend Helga and her Sardinian husband Massimo. We spend the days swimming and walking and catching up on news of greenie mates. We take naps in the early afternoons to escape the relentless heat. Jack and I lie on separate sides of our big bed. It's too hot to be touching. That's what I tell him.

For our last day on the island Helga hosts a Sardinian festa in our honour—a day-long party in the mountains. She collects the three of us from the beach house in her battered red station wagon, bottles of *vino rosso* clunking in the back among the kids' toys. Kris sits in the front, Jack and I are quiet in the back, belted in on opposite sides as Helga drives us west towards the flinty grey mountains of the inland.

We've been invited to Massimo's country property—a long, low whitewashed building with a tiled roof on a hundred hectares of scrubby hills—which has been in the family for generations. Massimo has the two rooms on the right, his uncle has the middle section and his sister's two rooms are on the left. There's a stone bench all the way around the outside wall of the house so you can find shade at any time of the day. Today will be scorching hot again, I can smell it.

We're the first guests to arrive, so we unpack the car and go for a walk up the dirt road behind the house. We wander past a couple of old Fiat Pandas rusting under an olive tree and stop to visit the pigpen. Behind the fence there is a sow and her litter; the piglets' father sniffing around outside the pen, snorting at us. Banished? Further along the track, in a crumbling concrete outbuilding, are more pigs and a keening black puppy. I want to pick up the puppy, but it won't let me near, and I'm surprised by my sudden tears.

When we return to the house more cars are pulling up, and the new guests are cheek-kissing and *ciao*'ing. Massimo has arrived with their two girls, six and eight, both of them with their father's black hair and their mother's tangled curls. He has also brought the carcass of a wild boar, shot for the occasion. Massimo hugs us all and introduces us to his best friend, a sexy balding man called Stefano. He wears his shirt unbuttoned to the waist and carries a guitar. I try not to stare at his flat brown belly.

Massimo's boar is in the oven and Stefano has brought a wild hare for stewing. The meat will take several hours to cook so while we wait, we drink red wine outside on the stone bench. A small Sardinian mountain man named Adolfo picks up Stefano's guitar and begins playing. He has very little sense of rhythm except when he sings traditional Sardinian songs in dialect, and then suddenly, miraculously, he can keep the beat. He tells me about the origins of this music while Jack, asking for a turn with the guitar, sits beside me, quietly picking out chords.

Sometime later another man arrives, drinks a lot of wine very quickly, then passes out on the couch. Stefano, who turns out to be a practical joker, beckons us all inside to watch while he ties the drunken man's legs together with an old cord and then ties the cord to a chair. Helga's two girls try to shake the prisoner awake and when this fails, they grab my hands and drag me outside to play. They bring out a box of watercolours and some old paintbrushes and white paper.

'What shall I paint?' I ask them in Italian. 'Animals!' they reply in unison. I paint a *guffo* (owl), an *elefante,* a *pecora* (sheep), and a *gallina* (chicken). When they ask for Australian animals I introduce them to kangaroos and koalas. Next we play a game called *nascondino*, which I assume means hide and seek, but their attempts to explain the complex rules to me in Italian go right over my head.

Helga comes outside to watch us. When the children wander away, she tells me about the Sardinian tradition of kidnapping. It's a popular form of extortion among the local bandits, apparently. Wealthy Sardinians often send their children to school with an armed guard. If their children *are* taken by bandits, the parents always pay the ransom. Helga grows teary as she tells me the story of one foolish Italian mainlander who wouldn't pay up, whose daughter was kept in a hole in the ground for months before being murdered. 'They stole my horse once,' Helga says, 'but I didn't care. So long as they don't touch our girls.' The girls have commandeered a piano accordion from one of the other visitors and are taking turns making seesawing noises.

'Do you have any children?' Helga asks me.

I consider offering her the long answer, but neither her English nor my Italian is up to it. I shake my head and wander away, looking for Jack. He's taken his camera and gone back up the dirt road behind the house to capture some close-ups of wildflowers. As I climb slowly towards where he is crouched by the side of the track, I have the strange sensation that he is actually getting further away from me. I pause, staring. He hasn't seen me yet and I watch him moving in closer to the flowers, arms bent awkwardly to hold the camera at the right angle. What does he think about in these moments of intense concentration? I've never known someone with such single-minded focus. He applies it equally to whatever task he's engaged in—brushing his teeth, shaving, planning a holiday, trying to get me pregnant, investigating IVF, remaining optimistic. I feel like a mess, in comparison, a wobbling mess of what-ifs. I hurry back down the hill before he sees me, resisting the temptation to run.

When I get back lunch is ready and a dozen people are seated at the long wooden table in Massimo's kitchen. As he carves up the boar Massimo speaks passionately about how important it is for Sardinian families to hold on to their culinary traditions and pass them on to their children, because their people are so few, so isolated, and so angry with the mainland Italians, especially the Romans, who've been invading their island in one form or another—most recently as loud summer tourists—since before Christ was born.

Jack misses out on the boar, but returns just in time for a bowl of hare stew. After the meal we move outside again to continue the music. Adolfo the mountain man sings more Sardinian songs, the others joining in when they know the words. I try to sing 'Dock of the Bay' while Jack plays guitar, but I forget half the words because the wine has been too good and too plentiful, and because I seem to be having trouble remembering anything at the moment. Jack has remained sober, carefully matching one glass of water for every wine. Kris, though, is happily drunk, mixing up his languages and creating accidental-on-purpose jokes in the gaps between German, English and Italian. Everyone except Jack is laughing. When he looks questioningly at me from the other side of the table, I turn away.

When the sun begins to set we pack everything up and clamber back into the red station wagon, the two children sitting on our laps in the back seat, their bony bottoms digging into our full bellies. As we drive towards the coast I try singing 'Waltzing Matilda' to them, but the words make no sense in this place. The eldest girl hands me her toy mobile phone and tells me it's a call from my great-grandmother. I play along. *'Ciao, biz-nonna, come stai* in heaven? How are you? Are you *confortevole* sleeping on those clouds?' The girls giggle at my mongrel sentences and then the younger one asks Jack and me a question in Italian. 'Where are your *bambini*?'

Jack doesn't understand. I will have to answer. But how do you explain that some children are not kidnapped by bandits, they simply disappear from an ultrasound screen like a light shadow fading on a retina?

—

It's 2019 and someone on Twitter has posed a challenge: 'Write a sad story in three words.' I click on the speech bubble and type *One blue line.*

ambivalence

IT'S LATE 2001 and I'm getting around with the aid of a walking stick. My spine has joined forces with my reproductive system, both of them determined to show me just how fallible a human body can be. A bulge in the lumbar region has become a prolapsed disc, resulting in numbness down the front of my left leg and searing pain down the back of it. The offending disc staged its prolapse within weeks of our return to Melbourne. Just as we were about to start investigating IVF, in fact.

The sadness that had dogged me during our overseas trip has also prolapsed, into depression. I have no job, no baby, and almost no mobility. My plan was to embark on a freelance career. A few short-term gigs have popped up—public interviews with authors, the occasional newspaper column or theatre review—but they all require energy and focus. Making a long-term life plan feels impossible when all I really want is for the pain in my leg to go away. I shuttle back and forth from home to the physiotherapist's office, waiting for something to budge. In between appointments I spend a lot of time lying facedown on the living-room rug, breathing deeply, hoping oxygen might be a miracle cure for nerve pain. With each breath release I create a miniature dust storm under the couch. Vacuuming is beyond me.

It's beyond Jack, too, at the moment. After our trip to Europe he's come back to a monstrous workload at the university. He leaves the house early and comes home late. During the long days part of me is glad to be free of us, together, but another part of me is waiting for him to fix all of this. While I wait, I think about the future. Specifically, a future for us without children. Just Jack and me. Would it be enough? Enough for what? As I shift around on the floor, trying to find relief, my imagination goes to places it's never been before. Railway tracks. Bloodstained baths. It's surprisingly easy to picture these scenes.

I have been to counsellors in the past, when the world has become ugly. Right now, the ugliness is overwhelming. I ask around and am given the name of a psychologist who might be able to help me see things differently. When I phone her, she's just had a cancellation so the following morning, after Jack has gone to work, I fold myself painfully into my little car and drive to the psychologist's office in the leafy eastern suburbs. She doesn't ask about the walking stick but gets straight down to business: why am I here?

Where to begin?

I tell her about the day my boss at the radio station invited me into his office for an unscheduled meeting. About how he couldn't look me in the eyes as he told me I was being sacked. About how I fled to a toilet cubicle and whimpered into my cupped hands.

I tell her about the miscarriages and how far I have drifted from Jack since the third one, and how much further we could drift if—or when—we fail again. About how afraid I feel when I think about the future.

I tell her about the prolapsed disc and how hard it has been to contain my rage with this treacherous body of mine.

When I tell her about the train tracks and the red baths she looks up from her notebook and directly into my eyes. 'How long have you been having these thoughts?'

'A while. Since the back injury. Maybe longer.' Maybe since Sardinia. I thought the trip to Europe would make things better, bring Jack and me closer. Instead, I found myself lying awake in the beach house by the Ligurian Sea, formulating escape plans.

She reads my mind. 'Are you having these thoughts because you can't think of another way out of your current situation?'

'I can't escape my body. I can't reverse time and get my radio career back,' I tell her. 'And I can't leave Jack. He's so good and kind. He doesn't deserve it. I'm trapped.' Not just good and kind. He's relentlessly optimistic. His optimism takes up so much space, there is no room for my sadness. Or my rage.

'Perhaps you're afraid of appearing not to be good and kind yourself,' she says quietly. 'Because the situation with Jack is the thing you *could* change, if you wanted to.'

Suddenly there is relief. Yes. I could jump ship. Float away in the wake, to another life. Leave my waiting, failing self and become someone else, someone who can stop trying to be good. Someone untethered. I'm filled with adrenaline. Fight or flight...and there is nothing for me to fight.

That afternoon I pack a suitcase and ring my mother to ask if I can stay with her and my stepfather for a few days. Then I lie facedown on the rug again, waiting for Jack to come home, trying to think of the words that will hurt him the least.

This is what I want to tell him. *Failure has drowned desire. Dread has drowned hope.* But he will think they can both be rescued. That he can save us if he is even more kind, and even more optimistic.

When he arrives home, I utter my carefully rehearsed sentences and Jack's face goes grey with shock. Mostly he is concerned about me. Where will I go? What about my wrecked back? How will he be able to look after me if I leave?

All I can say is *sorry—sorry—sorry—sorry—sorry—*

Four days later a plane flies into the World Trade Center in New York. I've been sleeping in the studio above the garage at my parents' house and learn of the terrorist attack when I turn on the old clock radio beside the bed. At first, I assume the news reports are part of an elaborate radio play, a 'War of the Worlds' for the new century. But no actor could conjure the sharp edge of panic in the newsreader's voice.

Without thinking I phone Jack. I cry, because everything is all wrong, everywhere. He tries to comfort me, but his kindness only makes everything worse. Maybe I have already become a bad person. Surely only a bad person could be so unkind to such a good person?

—

My mother loved A. A. Milne with the passion of a lifelong Anglophile. Growing up, I was expected to love him too. But it wasn't all Winnie the Pooh and marmalade for breakfast. One of the poems in *When We Were Very Young* has a child in a red coat striding along a pavement, instructing the reader on how to avoid being eaten by 'masses of bears'. Don't step on the lines. Keep in the squares. This is what good children do.

I have been keeping in the squares for years. Working hard. Eating well. Taking advice from experts. Having sex when instructed. But the bears haven't followed the rules. They've broken out of their cages and found me.

turbulence

PERHAPS I AM NOT a wholly bad person? At any rate, there are people to catch me when I leap. I become nomadic, house-sitting for friends, staying with my sister and her family. More work comes my way: small consultancies, editing jobs from mates, hosting gigs. Sitting at a desk is only just manageable and walking becomes harder and harder as the pressure on my spinal cord intensifies. One night, after hosting a public interview with a visiting author, I sneak away from the post-event dinner and lie on a bench seat in the back of the restaurant, sweating with agony. It's ridiculous. I should be in bed. Or in an ambulance. But I can't say no to any of these gigs. Each one offers me a scrap of evidence that I can take care of myself.

Jack calls, wanting to talk, so we meet up in a park— neutral territory. It's a mistake. The park is full of picnicking families. Older children bossing around younger siblings. Fathers teaching sons how to kick a footy. I turn my back on them and focus on the blades of spring grass that my fingers have picked and are now tearing into tiny pieces.

Jack still can't understand why I left. He thinks he must have done something wrong, and if I could just explain it to him, he might be able to fix it. As if the vision we'd had of our future can be stitched together like a ripped net. When I tell him how much I still care about him, it only makes things worse. We part with a hug and I can feel his shoulders trembling.

Eventually my leg gets so bad I wind up in hospital. Days pass in a fog of pain as I wait for scans, then for specialists to assess the scans. Part of me is relieved to be bedridden and dependent on the nurses for every little thing. I can't fix this by myself, no matter how hard I try. I want to beg the surgeon to take a knife to me.

Finally, the specialists agree that I need an operation. They put me to sleep and slice me open to remove the rogue bit of disc material pressing on my spinal cord. When I wake the fierce pain in my leg has been replaced by a fierce pain in my back that I know will fade eventually. The nurses bring me painkillers every four hours and bathe me with warm washers, and I appreciate the novelty of medical care that has nothing to do with my reproductive system.

After a week my sister Yoni picks me up from the hospital and installs me in her spare bedroom. My three-year-old nephew is delegated to bring me glasses of water, a responsibility he fulfils with great seriousness and very few spills. Slowly I learn to step carefully (not stride) as I wait for the wound to heal. Lying as still as possible on my nephew's backyard trampoline, soaking up the spring sunshine, I wonder if I'll ever be able to jump again. After months of limping, one of my legs is thinner than the other. Yoni cooks enormous meals, trying to feed me up.

One day I walk too far from my sister's house and can't get back. My body has reached its limit. No one is home at Yoni's place. Jack lives and works only a few kilometres away. I phone him and he comes to collect me. His face is still chalky from what I have done to him. As he drives me back to Yoni's, a question hangs in the air between us. I can almost smell it, a sour-sweet odour of hope and fear. When we arrive, I thank him but don't invite him in.

Two months after the surgery I move back into the bayside flat I vacated five years earlier to move in with Jack. Each day I stroll down to the beach and along the St Kilda pier, wishing it stretched all the way to the horizon so I could just keep walking. There are a dozen fishermen who seem to live on this pier. No matter what time of day I visit, they're sitting in the same spots, smoking the same brand of cigarettes, waiting for their luck to turn. Every now and then one of them reels in a piece of waterlogged plastic and curses the murky bay. I'm waiting for my luck to turn, too. Waiting to stop feeling cursed.

After months of being too scrambled to concentrate on anything much, I've begun reading again. I come across the word *apophasis*. Sounds like how my face has been feeling since I ended the relationship with Jack—apathetic, as if it can't be bothered smiling. But the dictionary tells me *apophasis* means 'the practice of describing something by stating which characteristics it does not have'.

How curious. Presence rendered by absence. Maybe this is how you capture the idea of loss—by describing what has gone. I start making a list.

> *Patience.*
> *Lungs full of air.*
> *Luxurious full body stretches.*
> *Giggling fits.*
> *The desire to dance.*
> *The dance of desire.*
> *Hope.*

dalliance

AS A CHILD I couldn't get enough of Cinderella. Who could resist the princess-in-waiting with the perfect feet? Both my feet were too long, and one was even longer than the other. I wanted dainty feet, like the girl with the broom. But there was a lot of meanness in Cinderella's world. The stepmother was a nightmare. And where the hell was Cinderella's father? Why didn't he protect her from all that meanness? Why didn't he snatch the broom from his daughter's dainty hands and give it back to the wicked stepmother—or better still, sweep the damn floor himself? Was Cinderella secretly hoping an alternative father-figure might come and rescue her?

Cinderella was the saddest, luckiest fictional character I'd met. All she ever wanted was to live happily ever after. When a prince showed up waving a glass slipper, she didn't stand a chance.

Tom the songwriter doesn't offer me a glass slipper. Instead, he starts sending me emails, strange missives from the glamorous world of rock'n'roll. I've long been a fan of his music, and anyway we've met several times in the past, so of course I reply. Over the next few months, we have rambling textual conversations about the songs he's been writing, the books we've been reading, the latest album he's recording. We move on to the pros and cons of fame, the recent end of his second marriage and, eventually, to where we might like to meet for lunch. I'm flattered by his attention. My sense of self-worth had deflated like a leaking balloon after I lost the radio hosting job. Now Tom's interest is making me feel interesting again.

After the lunch our emails get longer. We exchange opinions on Shakespeare and Austen, the poems we love, and where we might like to meet for dinner. After the dinner we start sending each other text messages, and after a while we send them in rhyming couplets, or in fake-Welsh spelling, minus the vowels. His texting gags make me laugh out loud, and I love to imagine mine doing the same for him. Each message, each little bit of wordplay, hauls me further out of the mire. I am no longer an underemployed, spinally challenged, single, childless woman approaching middle age. I am a special correspondent.

When Tom and I spend the night together I show him the scar from my back surgery. Then he shows me the scar from his vasectomy, explaining that he doesn't want any more children. For a moment I stop breathing. My body understands what this means. My brain, though, takes the information and quickly files it under *Not Now, Later*. I don't want to think about the future. It could be just as bad as the past. Right now, I want to live in the moment.

His life is crammed full, with siblings (seven), kids (three), ex-wives (two), other lovers (how many?), live gigs (so loud), recording sessions (so sweaty), songwriting sessions (so mysterious) and meetings with his accountant (why so many?). He lives only a couple of kilometres away from my flat, so after he's finished fitting all those other things into his day, he walks the darkening streets to my place, climbs the stairs and knocks gently on my back door. Sometimes, after dark, I go knocking on his front door instead and he cooks me pasta and pours me red wine and takes me to his bed.

On the nights when he's busy, I spend a lot of time wondering who else he might be cooking pasta for, who else might be walking barefoot up the long hallway of his cottage with a glass of red wine. I try to tell myself it doesn't matter, that this is temporary, something to replace the nothing. When, after a few months, he announces he is no longer seeing other women, it feels like winning first prize in a competition I don't recall entering. Then he tells me he loves me, and the other women fade away into the background.

But he adds this: 'I want to be loved deeply but held lightly.' There's a warning in his words. Depth I can do, but I've never been good at lightness, especially when it comes to love. I sense there might be trouble. Like the vasectomy, I file his strange phrase under *Not Now, Later.* I need this love affair more than I've ever needed anything. It's keeping me afloat.

It takes Tom's siblings a while to become curious about me. Over the decades they've seen the girlfriends come and go, and the wives, and they don't expect this latest one to last. They still speak often and fondly about his second wife. There are regular family barbecues at his place, and the guests often include his children and his siblings, his ex-wives and their parents and siblings, the ex-wives' other children and half-siblings, and sometimes even the ex-wives' siblings' children and partners. It makes my head spin, trying to figure out how they're all related.

His youngest children, two girls aged seven and nine, spend every second week with him. They are both petite and pretty with fashionable blonde streaks in their dark hair, and they sing harmonies in the back of his car. The girls are learning to play the piano and their father asks me to help them with their practice. We're tentative with each other at first. The spectre of Cinderella's wicked stepmother hovers in the back of my mind, the bossy task mistress. I try to imagine how the girls must feel, still living half their lives in the old family home where, instead of their small dark-haired mother, there's a tall blonde stranger leaning towards them over the keyboard.

Their mother is an actor and theatre director, and the girls have inherited her talents. They disappear into their bedroom for hours, making up plays. Sometimes they come to me and ask if I'll 'direct' them. When I admit I don't know how to direct plays, they're baffled. Isn't this what adults do? They trudge back to the bedroom and, as I listen to them arguing about how the play should be staged, I long for the courage to say yes to this thing I've never done before. Courage has been in short supply for a while now.

Sometimes in the night the younger daughter cries for her mother. Tom goes to her and, if she can't be comforted, he carries her down the hall and into our bed. As she drifts back to sleep in the warm space between us, I lie awake on the edge of the mattress, torn between wishing she was mine and wishing she wasn't here, so I could hold on to her father. But when they return home to their mother at the end of the week, I miss them. I wish the four of us could form a neat, tight little family unit, in the centre of the sprawling broken-and-blended clan I've attached myself to.

Tom's son from his first marriage is in his early twenties and although he's moved out of home, he visits often. He's easy to talk to, warm and curious, and immersed in music like his father. He's less cautious with me than his aunts and uncles are, and for that I am grateful.

After Tom and I have been together for about six months, his siblings finally begin to relax their guard. I'm working as a freelance journalist and some of them read my stories and email me their thoughts. They and their partners all have hungry minds, strong views and interesting jobs. Teachers, musicians, social workers, lawyers, linguists, activists, writers—vivid people, it seems to me, living vivid lives. I've never encountered a family this large with bonds of affection as strong as theirs. If there is competition between them, it's tempered with humour. If there's irritation with each other, it's kept under wraps for the sake of harmony. They're bound together by love, blood, in-jokes, sentimental songs and pride in each other—especially in their brother's musical success.

In their company I begin to feel vivid, too. This is a club I want to belong to. I could learn those in-jokes, sing those songs. But what to do about the blood? Tom has been very clear. He's in his late forties and he doesn't want to have any more children, which means no shared blood between us. I've given myself a 'sabbatical' from trying to have a child. At the end of the year I will figure out what to do. I'm only thirty-seven. There's still time. Even if I have to do this thing alone, I'll find a way.

—

It's late 2019 and I've been googling fertility statistics. A recent study compares women's ability to conceive in different age groups. Women aged thirty-eight to thirty-nine have a thirty per cent lower chance of conceiving compared to women aged thirty to thirty-one. Men's age matters too. It takes longer for partners of men over forty to conceive, and even longer if the men are over forty-five. The risk of miscarriage is higher for women whose partners are over forty-five, and the risk of 'genetic abnormalities' increases along with the parents' age.

There's a series of graphs on the website about the decline in IVF success rates with age. They're not easy to decipher but I get the picture. Every year a woman delays trying to get pregnant, her chances of having a child shrink.

This is not new information to me. I knew back then that my fertility was already problematic, even if I still didn't know why. I knew I was making things harder for myself by having a fertility sabbatical. But there were always the outliers—women in their early to mid-forties who were giving birth to healthy babies. Stories about these births often featured in the newspapers I was writing for. Miracle babies, they were called. Some women got lucky, which presumably meant any woman could get lucky. And after a run of bad luck, mine had finally turned. I had recovered from spinal surgery, made a new career for myself, and fallen in love. There was no reason to think my luck was about to run out.

parlance

IT'S LATE 2002 and time is speeding up. My working
life has become busy again, with newspaper columns and
theatre reviews to write, and singing rehearsals to attend.
Night after night I catch trams to theatres all over town and
then catch them back again, jumping off near the corner of
Tom's street and hurrying to his door. If he's not out playing
a gig, I usually find him reading a book in bed, waiting for
me. I tell him about the performance I've just seen and
then we start our own private ritual. In the absence of a
fertility-driven timetable, sex is revelatory. For years my
body has been a source of pain and disappointment, a faulty
vehicle that no medical mechanic has been able to fix. Now
it has become a source of pleasure and pride. I'm evolving
into a happy hedonist.

Tom travels a lot for work and sometimes, if my articles

have all been filed, I travel with him. There are weekends in beachside towns where his band is playing at the local pub. There are festival shows in other capital cities and, one weekend, a quick trip to Singapore. While he goes to afternoon soundchecks I wander the streets of whichever town we're in, staring in shop windows, walking along beach paths, watching seagulls squabbling on jetties, filling in time until we can be together again. Until I can step back into the role of The Songwriter's Girlfriend. There's so much goodwill coming my way simply because I am loved by someone whose work is admired by so many. The concert promoters who show me to my seat at Tom's gigs. The fans who want to get to know me, because it makes them feel like they'll know him better. The other songwriters who confide in me about how Tom's work has influenced theirs. It's addictive.

Sometimes I sense that I don't belong in this world. Backstage, at drinks with the band after the gig, words are tossed around that I've never heard before. Words like *zoners,* which Tom uses to refer to fans who try to get too close to him. And *cougars,* as in 'did you check out the cougars in the front row?' When I ask Tom what that one means, he changes the subject. I look it up online.

> A cougar is an older woman who frequents clubs in order to score with a younger man. The cougar can be anyone from an overly surgically altered wind-tunnel victim to an absolute sad and bloated horn-meister.

The contempt takes my breath away. Why such disgust?

Or is it fear? What do men find threatening about an older woman who enjoys sex with a younger man? Maybe it's a fear that the younger, fitter man may be colonising their sexual territory; or an uncomfortable reminder that their own mothers may still be sexually active. What would Dr Freud say? I'm thirty-eight years old. Even though Tom is ten years older than me, in the world of rock'n'roll that definitely makes me 'an older woman'.

The reminder of my age is also a reminder that I'm running out of time. My year-long sabbatical is over. I need to figure out what to do. The thought of giving Tom up is unbearable. Are these two things I want so badly—romantic love and motherhood—mutually exclusive? (I bet Cinderella and the prince had kids. As many as they wanted. No miscarriages. No medical interventions. I bet he had top-quality sperm and she had easy labours. That's part of the deal with *happily ever after*.) I start researching vasectomies and fertility.

There's a whole new vocabulary of alliterative multi-syllabic words out there that I've never heard before. *Vasovasostomy*, for example. This is option number one for a vasectomy reversal, and it involves reconnecting the two tubes that transport sperm out of the testicle. Then there's a *vasoepididymostomy*, which reconnects the coiled section of the sperm ducts (*epididymis*) to the transport tube (*vas deferens*). After a while I give up trying to memorise these scientific names and privately nickname the two reversal methods the *Vincero* (with apologies to *Verdi*) and the *Viva*

Las Vegas (with apologies to Elvis). The best news about the two procedures is that after your partner has had one, you can (try to) have a baby naturally by having as much sex as you like. *Va-va-voom!*

If a reversal is not your bag, there's another option called *sperm aspiration*, which has nothing to do with aspiring to produce top-notch sperm. This charming procedure involves sticking a needle into a testicle and suctioning out the sperm that's stuck in there, post-vasectomy, with no escape route. Just reading about it makes me wince. It's usually done under local anaesthetic, but it can be painful afterwards. The other catch is that this method requires you to be on an IVF program; the aspirated sperm is used to fertilise the woman's harvested eggs in a laboratory. *Sperm aspiration,* I read, is highly successful when used with IVF, 'especially if your (female) partner is under thirty-five years old'. Whoops. I missed that boat three years ago.

Still, there are ways and means. All I need to do now is persuade Tom to try one of these vexatious variables on a vasectomy reversal.

limerence

IN 2019 I come across a new word: *limerence*. The friend who introduces me to this word says it describes how you feel when you're madly in love. My dictionary has a slightly different take: *limerence* is 'an involuntary interpersonal state that involves an acute longing for emotional reciprocation, obsessive-compulsive thoughts, feelings, and behaviours, and emotional dependence on another person'.

Limerence. What a sound it makes, an onomatopoeic melange of *shimmering liminal immanent elysian deliverance*. I'm showing you what I couldn't see way back then, because of *limerence*.

⁓

It's late spring 2002 and I'm gently trying to persuade Tom to change his mind. There has been some calm and considered dialogue. At least, that's how it would sound to anyone listening. I've tried to keep any emotion out of my voice, tried to argue with logic and rationality. Fortunately, no one can hear my plaintive interior monologue during these conversations—*if he really loved me he would do this thing with me—why was he willing to have children with his two ex-wives but not with me—can't he see how much I love his children and how much his children would love our child—can't he understand how impossible it is for me to choose between loving him and being a mother?*

He tells me he wants his freedom. 'I've been bringing up kids for twenty years,' he says, 'and there are at least another ten years before the girls are grown. I don't want to be tied down anymore. What if I want to go and live in Spain for a year?'

This is the first time I've heard him talk about going to Spain. *Couldn't I come with you?* Or *couldn't we?* I don't ask, perhaps because I don't want to hear the answer.

He seems to think we could stay together even if I had someone else's child. In his vision of this future, I would live separately with the baby and he would continue to visit me (or us). I try to imagine myself and my crying baby as guests at the family barbecues, circling the perimeter of that genetic pool, always the outsiders. It's not what I want. I want to be with him, in the middle of the pool, forever. Our conversations on this topic go nowhere, but at least he hasn't shut them down completely.

One afternoon I'm sitting on the bed reading when he

comes into the room holding his guitar. 'I wrote a new song and I want to play it to you.'

I put down my book, adjust the pillows behind me and sit up straighter. The first listener: still gives me a ridiculous thrill. He perches on the edge of the bed and adjusts the capo on the strings. The opening chords are tentative. He makes a mistake and starts again.

From the first few lines, it seems this is going to be a love song about a long-legged girl. My legs are stretched out on the bed, one foot lightly touching his knee. *It must be me.* He makes another mistake, corrects himself and continues. Is he nervous? The scene in the song is post-coital, the couple breathless. I'm scarcely breathing now myself.

The couple go all around the world together. The woman doesn't believe in God. *Just like me, me, me.* He's looking down, concentrating on his fingers. Good. I don't want him to see the colour in my face. Then he sings the second verse. The woman wants a baby. She's running out of time. She needs to find herself a man who wants the same.

An icy wave washes over me.

He's still singing, something about the woman setting his heart aflame, but I'm finding it hard to take in any more words. *How could he?*

When the song ends there is silence. His face is still turned away from me.

'You can't do that.' My voice is louder than it needs to be. 'You can't just take that and put it in a song.' At last he looks up, his eyes wary.

'That is mine,' I say. 'My story. My pain. You can't. You can't tell the world about it.'

He sighs. He's been here before. 'It's just a song.'

'But everyone will know, or assume, that it's us. You know they do that. You've complained to me about it, how people think all your songs are autobiographical. And it *is* about us. I don't want them to know. It's no one else's business.'

Now he's staring at me. 'Sian, you hooked up with a writer. This is how it works.' He sounds like a lawyer, trying to persuade a client to give up a hopeless case.

I move my foot away from his knee. My words are slow, my voice unnaturally calm. 'I'm asking you. Please. I don't want you to put that in a song and sing it to the world. We haven't worked this out yet. I don't know if we're going to be able to. At the very least, can you wait? Put it aside until this is behind us?'

He leans forward as if to kiss me—*kiss it better, like I'm a child*—but now I'm off the bed and standing rigid in the doorway.

'No,' he says. 'I have to be able to write what I want to write. I'm going to use it for the next album. But I wanted you to hear it first. Besides,' he adds, grinning now, 'don't you want to be immortalised?'

The question pulls me up. Is this what he thinks his songs are—bids for immortality? *Is* immortality what I want? Is that why I'm so determined to have a child—so a part of me can live forever?

You already have immortality—this is what I want to tell him—*through your children. Your children may have children, and those children may have their own children. That's the only kind of immortality I'm interested in.*

But the penny has finally dropped. He's made up his mind. He doesn't want to have a child with me. And yes—as the song says—I'm running out of time.

exuberance

IT'S SUMMER 2018 and I'm at a surf beach on the west
coast of Victoria. I'd planned to have a quick swim and
then walk the dog, me zipped up in my wetsuit, the two
of us hermetically sealed in our solitude. But on the beach
a family is sitting at a picnic table: a man, two women and
two girls. As I walk past them the girls spring up from the
bench seat and race towards the dog.

'Oh, can we pat her?' Jazzy is instantly ready for play,
leaping around them and barking. 'Can we chase her?'

Dark eyes, early teens, tight blue jeans, but still children
when it comes to dogs and the chasing of them. I laugh
and laugh at their dancing game, grit kicking up around
them, Jazzy swerving so the girls lunge and fall in the soft
dry sand.

At the picnic table the two women in headscarves nod

and smile at us, as the girls pick themselves up and come towards me.

'What's your dog's name?' The older one speaks in a rush. 'We had a dog, he was a Jack Russell cross, we loved him so much, but we couldn't look after him, Mum said, so we gave him away to one of Mum's clients, but we miss him.' And now they're off again, sprinting after Jazzy to the water's edge and back.

'Are we holding you up?' the older girl asks.

'No, I'm just about to have a swim, you go right ahead.' I inch my way through the biting waves, glancing back at the dancing trio. Oh, to be able to run like that still, to fall with impunity, to have teenage daughters to run with, fall with, laugh with.

As soon as I come out of the water they're by my side again, telling me more stories about the Jack Russell, about puppy school, about their aunt who's come from Turkey to visit them. 'Where do you live?' I ask.

'In Victoria. Oh, you mean what street—no, what suburb?' They look at each other, shrugging. They don't know where they live. They live at home, with Mum and Dad. That is enough.

In between quizzing me they speak to each other in Turkish and I love the way it rushes from their lips, all sibilant like the waves behind them. Then they ask me that question. 'Do you have children?'

There is a pause—the first pause—in the conversation. Finally I say, 'Jazzy is like my child.'

Then on they go, telling me their names are Joozher and Azra, laughing about how, if you put their names together, you'd get something like Jazzy. They talk about the boys who break the rules at their high school, and more about their lost dog, and then somehow it is time for me to go, because I cannot keep them.

I walk slowly up the hill to the borrowed beach house, full of their beauty and openness and unknowingness.

Later in the evening I make myself walk back down the hill to the pub, but it's a mistake. It is all and only families, clusters of kids being herded and fed, and nowhere for me to sit. I lean against the balcony railing and sip my wine and fiddle with my phone and watch the children, the easy chatting, the blurred lines between family units, and today it is too hard.

So I take my glass and head back to the beach, where I kneel in the sand, gulping the wine and staring at the grey ocean. When the wine is gone I walk home fast, waiting to feel Jazzy's sandy paws jumping at my knees.

—

It's 2019 and people are debating why fewer Australian women are having children. The Bureau of Statistics reports that the birth rate in the last couple of years hasn't been this low since the turn of the century. Between 1976 and 2018 the proportion of couples without children increased from twenty-eight to thirty-eight per cent. An opinion writer in one of the weekend newspapers claims that childless women are 'opting for fur-babies' because they're 'scared of lifelong responsibility'. I look up from the newsprint and watch the small black dog chewing on a sock at the end of my bed. Sometimes I call her 'baby', it's true. But still. When it comes to parenting, she wasn't my first choice of species.

Maybe the women this writer is denigrating don't have as much choice as she thinks they do. It's not hard to find some relevant statistics. Around twenty-five per cent of the Australian population currently live alone. About two million Australians are currently single, and not all of them by choice. Infertility affects about one in six couples in this country. For same-sex couples, finding a way to have a child together can be quite the challenge. And if some women *are* actively choosing not to have children, maybe there are reasons other than selfishness.

According to a recent survey by the Australian Conservation Foundation, a third of Australian women are reconsidering their plans to have children because they believe climate change has created 'an unsafe future'. Maybe not having children feels like a selfless choice for these women. Maybe, as well as fearing for their children's future, they worry about the impact on the natural world if they produce more resource-sapping humans. Maybe it's not freedom from responsibility these women crave, but freedom from guilt. Or from fear.

I knew the future could be unsafe three decades ago, when I was campaigning on global warming for the ACF. But I wanted those children, more than anything. Maybe because three decades ago—two decades ago—one decade ago—there was still time to make the world safer. There was still hope.

inference

SOME THINGS STAY in your memory forever.

Scene one: I'm on a group trip to the snow. Lying on a bed in the mezzanine of the ski hut, I overhear two women below having a conversation about me. One of them has only recently met me, and she's telling her friend she's surprised to discover she actually likes me. 'Childless women,' she says, 'are usually so selfish.'

Scene two: Outside a polling booth on election day I'm handing out how-to-vote cards. A man I used to work with is standing nearby, handing out cards for a different party. He's asking me about my current working life. 'Of course,' he states confidently, 'you're obviously one of those women who chose to have a career rather than be a mother.'

Scene three: At a lunch gathering with friends, a woman I've known for twenty years is quizzing me about my desire to have a child. 'Maybe,' she says, 'you only wanted to have children because society told you that you should.'

Selfish Career Woman or Helpless Victim of Peer Pressure—which is it to be?

Former Australian prime minister Julia Gillard would be familiar with those stereotypes.

> *Quote one:* In 2006 Liberal Senator Bill Heffernan said publicly that Julia Gillard was unfit for leadership because she was 'deliberately barren'.

> *Quote two:* In 2010 Liberal Senator George Brandis said Julia Gillard was 'very much a one-dimensional person' who 'doesn't understand the way parents think about their children' because she 'has chosen not to be a parent'.

> *Quote three:* In 2011 former Labor Party leader Mark Latham said Prime Minister Gillard lacked empathy and was 'wooden' because of her decision to remain childless—a choice which inevitably meant 'you haven't got as much love in your life'.

Right, then. Let's add Loveless Sociopath to the list of stereotypes, shall we?

persistence

IT'S THE END OF 2002. I'm thirty-eight years old and I still want to have a child. Time to do something about it. I force myself to think clearly about my options. None of them is appealing.

> *Option one:* Leave Tom, try to find another partner who wants to have children, and try to get pregnant.

I can't leave this relationship. It's the best thing in my life right now. I can't imagine falling in love with anyone else ever again. Scratch option one.

> *Option two:* Stay with Tom but try to adopt a child as a single person.

Do I want to adopt someone else's child? Through all these long years of trying to have a baby, my fantasies have always involved a baby who has something of me in them.

But why? And what does 'something of me' mean? I study the way Tom's features have reproduced themselves, slightly morphed, in his three children. The wide-set brown eyes of his younger daughter. The loose-limbed athletic grace of his older daughter. His son's uncanny ability to remember numbers. His older daughter's love of stories. His younger daughter's shyness. The quick reflexes of his son when he plays tennis. Their father is there, just under the skin, in all of them.

And my own father? What is there of Glen lying under my skin? All I have learnt about him comes from some black-and-white photos and a few stories told by my mother. I know he was shy, like me. Tall and fair, like me. In love with music, like me. I have been told how very like him my brother is—tall, funny, gentle, sporty. Do I want a child who has something of my lost father in them?

One of the stories told and retold in our family is about the day my small dark-haired mother went out walking with her three blonde children and was stopped by a stranger, who exclaimed, 'What lovely children! Whose are they?' Sometimes I'm mistaken for being the mother of Tom's daughters. In a café a woman at the next table stares at the four of us, before leaning over and saying with a confident smile, 'Well, they obviously take after their mother more than their father!' It's a bittersweet compliment. But this much is undeniable: I want to be able to see myself in another. See my nose or my chin, my father's nose and chin, replicated in my child. Is it narcissism, a craving for a miniature version of myself? Or is it just how parents are?

I do some research and discover that, although adoption is legal for single people in most Australian states and territories, it's currently only permitted 'in special circumstances'. Those circumstances are not specified in the relevant legislation, but in practice, I learn, single people can only adopt children with 'special needs'. Children who are designated 'special needs' include those older than twelve months, those with a disability and those who may have experienced abuse or neglect.

I wonder whether I would be a good parent to such a child. I've had no experience with managing the needs of children with a disability, or with a history of trauma. What if this turned out to be something I couldn't do well? I might make things worse for one of these children. Or are these lame excuses? Maybe I'm just not selfless enough to take on the responsibility for someone who would require more of my time and energy than I wanted to give, and whose rights I might have to fight for, alone, as a single parent.

When I was a child, and my mother was researching for her PhD on autism, we spent several summers camping with the families of children on the spectrum. Many of these children had severe autism and they were often distressed and agitated. I saw how challenging it was for the parents to care for these children, and it frightened me.

I had other fears around adoption. I'd read stories about Romanian orphans adopted by naive American couples after the Iron Curtain came down and the tyrant Ceausescu was removed from power. In these orphanages naked infants were fed watered-down gruel and left to rot in overcrowded rooms, their physical, emotional and intellectual growth stunted by neglect, deprivation and abuse. There was no one to offer them love, no one to see them, smile at them, to hold them in mind. They were born into trauma. I read about the adopting parents' bafflement when these 'rescued' children failed to attach to anyone in their new family, and how, as those children grew older, the cruelty they'd endured early in their lives later manifested as rage and misery.

There'd been another frightening example of adoption closer to home. As a young teenager I earned pocket money by babysitting. In one family there were two children who'd been adopted from overseas. When their parents went out for dinner parties, I changed the children's nappies, fed them, played with them and read to them before they slept. Sometimes I imagined a future in which I had my own toddlers to feed and play with and tuck up in bed. Years later I learned that one of those adopted children was diagnosed with schizophrenia in early adulthood. They'd been violent towards the parents and spent much of their young adulthood moving in and out of psychiatric institutions. Their birth mother, I also learned, had suffered from the same mental illness, which was why the child had been offered up for adoption.

Individual anecdotes: not statistics, not science, not reliable evidence. But logic rarely trumps personal experience. Bad things had happened with people I knew; bad things might also happen if I adopted someone else's child. And if they did, I might not be able to cope alone.

I can judge myself kindly or harshly on all these questions but it makes no difference to how I feel about solo adoption. I don't want to do it. Scratch option two.

> *Option three:* Give up on the idea of having a child and try to be content with being Tom's partner and an intermittent stepmother to his three children.

If I sacrifice my desire to have a child for the sake of staying in the relationship, I might always wonder if the sacrifice was worth it. Will my imaginary child frown and shake their head every time Tom and I argue? And if we break up, maybe part of me will blame Tom for my childlessness.

One of the fairytales I read as a child was called 'The Little Mermaid'. This is what I remember: the mermaid falls in love with a human and is offered the chance to stay with him, leaving the sea and making her home on land. But there's a catch: she must give up her mermaid tail in exchange for human feet. Every step she takes will feel like walking on broken glass.

I don't want to spend the rest of my life with Tom regretting the steps I've taken—or not taken—to be with him. This is not his fault. He has a right to his freedom. Our timing is off. If we'd met ten years earlier, perhaps we could've tried to have that child together. But he doesn't want another one, and the last thing any child needs is a father who never wanted them to exist. Scratch option three.

Option four: Stay in the relationship but look for a friend or acquaintance who will donate sperm so I can try to have a child.

Is this my best option—find a willing sperm donor? Someone I like, someone who likes me, who would be happy to help? I have a friend, a single man, who's confided to me in the past that he hopes to have children one day. I invite him to come for a walk along the beach path, and as we wander past the rollerbladers and the dog walkers I explain my dilemma to him. When I get to the part about trying to find a friend who might help me have a child, he goes quiet. We walk in near silence back towards my flat. In the driveway I grit my teeth and ask the question.

He grimaces and makes an awkward joke about what a terrible father he'd be. When I reassure him he wouldn't have to be an active father, he makes another joke and farewells me, then dashes off up the street. I feel like a beggar.

Not long afterwards I describe this scene to another old friend, a married man with three sons. There's no hidden agenda. I've never considered asking him. Without prompting, though, he immediately offers to be a sperm donor for me. I thank him and tell him I'll need some time to consider his generous offer.

Over the coming days I try to imagine what it would be like—for me, for the child, for my friend—and for his wife. She's kind and empathetic. It could be hard for her to express any misgivings about her husband's offer. If I did have a child with the help of his 'donation', what would that mean for her, and for their sons? Would we be a kind of family, a sprawling thing like Tom's entourage of ex-wives, children and their half-siblings? Or would I be an awkward addendum to my friend's neat nuclear unit? What responsibilities would we all have for each other—and for the children? The more I think about it, the more complicated it seems. I reluctantly decline my friend's offer. Scratch option four.

> *Option five:* Stay with Tom and try to have a child as a solo parent using IVF and anonymous donor sperm.

This is my last, and my least-worst, option. It will cost a lot of money. The system is unfair. Many people can't afford it. I'm not wealthy, but I have some savings that could at least get me started. I call my gynaecologist.

dependence

IT'S 2018 and I'm reading an essay by a neonatal psycho-therapist who has been visiting Australian immigration detention centres. She's been trying to help asylum-seeker parents engage their babies in play. Encouraging them to do what most parents do without thinking. Smile at their babies. Talk to them in singsong voices. Wave toys in front of their googly eyes. Show them how to grab things and hold on for dear life. How to take control. How to feel safe.

The psychotherapist says newborn babies learn to smile by watching their parents smile. They learn to feel joy by seeing joy on the looming faces of their mothers and fathers. They learn the freedom of play when they are played with. But after years of uncertainty, these mothers and fathers have had the joy leached out of them. First, the psychotherapist says, the babies fixate on their parents' faces, trying to connect.

Then they give up. Their faces become immobile. The psychotherapist says that when she waves a toy in front of them, the babies turn away.

Not long after reading the essay by the neonatal psycho-therapist I'm in my mother's study, trying to sort out a problem with her laptop for her. Her desk is littered with scribbled notes, the mysterious hieroglyphics of an ageing mind. Words have been leaving her lately, like those fish you try to grab when you're snorkelling. So close, then slipping away at the last second. I find a piece of scrap paper on which my mother has written these words: *SP fixated on feedback.*

I've always signed off my letters and emails to her *lots of love, SP.* Is it me? It must be. *Am* I fixated on feedback?

When I was three months old my mother watched my father disappear under the surf. She had three young children to care for and no secure income, and was living a thousand miles from the rest of her family. Margot was plunged into an intense state of shock and fear. If a neonatal psychotherapist had visited our depleted family in the months following my father's death, what clinical notes might they have made?

> The widowed mother has sole responsibility for three small children. She is caring for the baby's basic needs but is not currently able to smile at her, or express joy. The baby seems anxious and hypervigilant, fixated on her mother's face, trying to connect. The anxiety and hypervigilance could be the baby mirroring her mother's emotions. Or perhaps the roles are reversed, and the baby is trying to care for

her mother's emotional needs, to ensure her own will be met.

There are very few photos of me as a baby. There's one I've seen in a yellowing news clipping, in which I'm shrouded in a soft blanket, held tight in the arms of a dark-haired woman who's standing at the sea's edge, waiting for her husband to resurface. There's one of me propped up on my big sister's knees, staring anxiously off to the side. There's another one of me at six months old, lying on my belly, head raised, worried eyes staring up and out, trying to take it all in. Trying to work out how to control something. Or someone.

I never gave up, never stopped trying to erase my mother's sorrow. Never stopped trying to fix things for her. Anything to make her smile. Visits, letters, emails, stories, jokes, meals, gifts, academic achievements, musical achievements, professional achievements. Anything for approval. Anything to make a connection. *Fixated on feedback.* Mired in a state of infantile dependency, desperate to connect.

Is this what I was like with Tom, too?

I watch children at the beach, playing in the shallows, jumping the waves, turning to check that a parent is watching. 'Did you see, did you see, did you see?' they call. This is the urgent plea at the heart of limerence. *See me.*

pretence

IN 2003 I published an anonymous article about embarking on solo IVF. Re-reading it a decade and a half later, it seems my story was not entirely accurate. Why did I fudge the truth? Who was I trying to convince?

> *I'm jogging around the local park and watching the men who are dashing past at twice my speed. I'm trying to work out their height and what colour eyes they have. There's nothing sexual in my gaze.*

Not true. Back then, when it came to men, my gaze was almost always sexual, as if the sexual energy between Tom and me radiated out over them all.

> *I'm wondering if one of these men could be the person whose profile I've been reading and re-reading since an IVF counsellor handed it to me a few days ago. I know it's*

ridiculous, because I have no idea where that man—who describes himself as five foot ten inches tall, blue-eyed and a 'regular jogger'—actually lives, let alone whether he jogs in a park, along a beach or at a gym. Nevertheless I am intensely curious. After all, one of these anonymous joggers could end up being the father of my child. I'm nearly forty years old, financially secure, currently single, with a history of medical infertility, and I want to have a child.

Not quite. I was a freelancer with a mortgage, and I wasn't single. I was hopelessly entangled with a man who didn't want to have a child with me. But yes: fertility was not one of my core competencies.

At the moment it seems that the only way I can attempt to do this is by using donor sperm in conjunction with in vitro fertilisation.

Not strictly true. I could have taken up my friend's offer of some sperm. Or I could have done some more asking around—other friends, acquaintances, friends of friends— 'Got any spare spermatozoa for a desperate woman?'—if I had not prized my dignity so highly.

Unless and until the Federal Government introduces new legislation to prevent me from achieving my goal, I meet the legal requirements for accessing that sperm. So the IVF counsellor has given me a handful of donor profiles to choose from. I feel deep regret and sadness that I am unable to conceive in the way most women do—within a stable relationship and without medical intervention. But at the

same time I'm feeling pretty good, because at least I have an
option, even if it's one with a fairly poor statistical success rate.

Feeling pretty good? About the fact that my partner didn't
want to help me have a child? Not so much.

Above all, I am deeply grateful to the handful of men in
this state who are currently offering their semen to women
like myself.

Yes. That much was true.

Trying to decide which donor to put at the top of my prefer-
ence list, though, is one of the strangest and most challenging
tasks I've ever been set. The information on the form is
simultaneously much more than I expected to be offered and
incredibly limited. These men want, and deserve, absolute
anonymity—at least until any child that results from their
sperm donation reaches the age of eighteen. So I am told their
age, weight, height, hair and eye colour, current occupation,
religion, and some information about their family's medical
history. There are a couple of lines on the form for them
to describe their own personality and the reasons they are
participating in the sperm donor program.

All true, as far as I can recall.

Compared to the amount of information most married women
have about the potential father of their child, though, it's
almost nothing. And yet perhaps that's not an appropriate
comparison. After all, I am not choosing a person with whom
I will share a home and build a family. I am not choosing a

lover. I am choosing a sperm donor. So which criteria should
I use in making that choice?

I have always hated that term 'build a family'—why did I use it? As if a family is like Jenga: wooden blocks piled on top of each other until one is pulled out from near the bottom and they all come tumbling down.

Do I care that one of the men says he jogs regularly? Does
the fact that I also jog regularly mean that at least we have
something in common, and does that matter when it comes
to choosing a donor?

Was I really jogging regularly? Only two years before this I'd had spinal surgery. I remember feeling tired all the time. I remember marching along the beach path, ruminating about Tom's intransigence. One day I bumped into an acquaintance, a woman my age, and in the icy sea wind her story tumbled out—she'd just been dumped by her boyfriend, she was desperate to have kids, and was considering putting her eggs 'on ice'. As she wept into a handkerchief, I pulled all the right faces, but said nothing to her about my own situation. Was I ashamed?

Or am I attracted to that option because it probably means
the donor is a fit and healthy person, and ideally I'd like
a healthy child?

Ideally. Sounds like I'm choosing a couch.

And what about education levels? If I was 'falling in love'
it would probably be with someone who had a similar level

of education to myself, simply because we would speak more of the same language. But I won't be talking to this person, so why should it matter if the sperm donor left school at sixteen? I know that school-leaving age is no measure of intelligence.

True. My stepfather, one of the smartest people I know, had to leave school early to go to work.

Then again, why am I assuming that intelligence should be a criterion of choice? Smart people aren't necessarily happier than less smart people, and I'm no modern-day eugenicist, trying to create a super-kid. Above all I want a child who is happy.

Prior, Prior, pants on fire. Back then, one of the attractions of having a child with Tom was the idea that the child might be as smart as him.

So perhaps I should ignore the information about education levels and move on to the self-description. That might help me to predict what kind of temperament a child conceived with this sperm might have. I wonder about the man who simply describes himself as 'ordinary'. Is he shy, private, modest, or does he lack self-esteem? If he lacks self-esteem, is that because of his genes or because of his upbringing? I admire modesty but I myself am shy, and who needs two genetic doses of shyness?

No wonder I went on to write a book about shyness. But yes: an accurate reflection of what I thought back then.

Another donor uses a long list of adjectives to describe himself, some of which are inherently contradictory. After all, 'relaxed' and 'driven' don't usually go together. Does that mean he's complex and interesting, or not taking the task of self-description seriously? Is he a bit of a joker, and does that mean his child would have a good sense of humour? I'm madly trying to read between the lines, and yet I still don't know what I'm looking for.

So I move on to health histories. If your health prognosis influences your chances of being happy, perhaps I should be choosing the man with the healthiest genes. All of the donors describe themselves as being very healthy, with no chronic medical conditions or known genetic problems. However, I have no way of verifying the accuracy of this information. I assume these men are being completely honest, but that could simply be because I usually assume the best about people's motives until I'm proven wrong. I am curious about the reasons behind these men's decisions to donate. Offering a stranger the chance to conceive and bear your genetic offspring is such a profound choice. None of them were paid for their donation.

Is this true? In the early days of sperm donations, young blokes were apparently paid good money for a wank. I bet they couldn't believe their luck.

Most say that they had heard about the shortage of donors for single infertile woman and wanted to help out. Some have had children using IVF and wanted to share the joy that this has brought them.

108

'Share the joy'? Why is our language about children littered with these soggy clichés?

> *One says his primary motive is helping others but adds that he also likes the idea of passing on his genes even if he never has children of his own. As I read through these reasons, I bless them all for their altruism, but hesitate at the man who wants his genes to live on. Is this a kind of Darwinian desire to keep your genes circulating in the gene pool? I can't deny, though, that one of the many reasons I want to try to give birth to my own biological child, in preference to adoption, is because I, too, like the idea of my genes living on. He's just being honest, and that's another quality I admire.*

Yes, that's true. Well done me, admitting to my selfish evolutionary imperative.

> *After reading every profile several times over, I find myself no closer to choosing a preferred donor. Am I trying too hard to control this situation? The truth is, I have very little control and very little choice, over either the father of my potential child or the outcome of my attempts to conceive using IVF. I can try not to worry about other people's judgments about my long and deeply considered choice. I can try to stay as healthy as possible to give my body the best chance of having a baby. I can build a network of supportive friends and relations to help me through the process, and to be a loving family for that baby, should I succeed.*

Such optimism. Or was it hubris?

Maybe it really doesn't matter which donor I choose. I don't know if there's a gene for generosity, but all of these sperm donors are generous people, and what better quality could I hope to pass on to a child?

At least one of these sentences turned out to be true.

⁓

It's winter 2018 and I've been making a list of things I've missed.

Holding a small hand at the traffic lights.
Fudging the answers to tricky questions ('why do spiders have eight legs?').
Applying a bandaid to an invisible wound.
Wrapping a warm beach towel around shivering shoulders.

Too sentimental? Don't worry. I have a less cloying list.

Being woken up too early for a decade.
Dealing with whingeing in supermarket checkout lines.
Catching every cold.
The inescapability of it all.

I'm trying to make myself feel better about this terrible freedom.

Last night on the TV news there was a story about a Victorian mother of four who was murdered so that a childless woman could keep those four children for herself. What strange logic—or madness—lay behind this scenario? Did she believe you could simply step into the mother's shoes, become the bandaid applier, the bedtime book reader, the school-lunch maker? Were children like kittens in a pet shop window for her—choose the ones you want and take them home? Had she been observing those children's mother, judging her, persuading herself that she would be a better mother? Or had she felt the same relentless undertow of longing that I'd felt, and finally been unable to resist it?

imminence

IT'S NEARLY CHRISTMAS, 2002. I'm still feeling tired most of the time, and I'm missing Tom, who's touring overseas again. I spend hours writing him long emails, confessing my trepidation about the IVF mountain I'm about to climb—solo. Having chosen the sperm donor, it's time to sign the forms. But part of me hasn't entirely abandoned the fantasy of Tom and me doing this together. I decide to try one last time to change his mind.

In a late-night email, I paint a picture of us sharing a life together—Tom, me, our child, his other children—all joined together by blood and love, words and music. I remind him of the risk of us fragmenting into separate units: me and the baby alone in my apartment, him and his extended family bustling in and out of his home in the next suburb. It's the most vulnerable letter I've ever written. After re-reading it half-a-dozen times, I press *send* and go to bed.

The next morning I head straight to the computer, nauseous with hope. No response. I check the outbox to make sure I've actually sent the email. Nausea turns to hot terror as I read the address. I've sent it to the wrong person. It's gone to someone else whose name starts with T. A newspaper editor.

Fuck fuck fuck fuck fuck!

I leap up from the desk and pace around the flat, hyper-ventilating. What if the editor has read my email? What if he's read it out to others? What if he's forwarded it to their entertainment reporter? I can see the headline now: *Songwriter's Sweetheart Solicits Sperm.*

I force myself to sit down at the desk again and re-read the email. It's vulnerable, intensely so, but it's not humiliating. I'm not begging. Maybe my dignity is salvageable, even if the email does get out. And maybe I'm underestimating this editor. He's always been ethical in our past dealings. I take a deep breath and start writing to him. I explain what's happened and ask if he could *please* delete the wrongly addressed email without reading it. This time I *am* begging. Then I wait.

One long hour later the editor responds. He assures me that he *hasn't* read the first email and that he *has* deleted it. Can I believe him? What other option do I have? Meanwhile Tom still hasn't received my urgent missive. He'll be asleep now on the other side of the world. I cut and paste my original message into a new email, add a sentence about how

I'm 'about to sign the form to go ahead with donor sperm', and send it carefully to the correct address. Then I wait.

Twelve hours later I receive a response. The subject line reads 'Before you sign that form'. My eyes can't scan the text quickly enough to keep up with my thudding heart. It's a long email, but the most important sentences are at the very end. 'I tried to give the idea of you having a child alone some time to settle but it still doesn't sit right with me. Should we keep talking?'

incandescence

MEMORIES ATTACH to emotions like jockeys to race-horses, galloping off into the future together. That's what the brain experts say.

Manly Beach, Sydney, the end of 2002: I thought I would remember every moment of every day of that week. It was the happiest week of my life. The week my object of desire finally seemed to be within reach. I should be able to replay it still, even after all these years, but only traces of the truth remain.

Truth was important that week. That was the week that proved there can be too much truth.

But before that there was joy. Heat softening everything, inside and out. Pliable flesh, the sweet stink of sunscreen. If joy left a trail there would be glittering tracks up and down the seafront.

Walking the beach path together, salty skin-on-skin, my left arm around his brown shoulders, his right hand resting on my rolling hip. Dunking ourselves in the sea. Hands hidden under wave froth, caressing thighs. Sitting back to back in the burning sand, reading books, matching the rhythm of our breathing so we rock gently back and forth.

The bland hotel room with a double bed and a single one. The afternoon we both try to get some work done, sitting on separate beds with laptops. It lasts about seven minutes. Over the gap he jumps and onto the single bed with me. We can't stop.

Dinner at a swanky beachside restaurant on New Year's Eve. After midnight, in the shadow of the bluestone seawall, clothes loosened, fucking standing up to bring in the new year.

My helpless, hapless gratitude. My weak-limbed relief. The deep seismic shock of discovering that everything you ever wanted could be suddenly granted—a grand ocean-quaking love, and the possibility of this love producing a child.

He has said yes.

Waking in the night, breathing in his fennel scent, I am making our perfect child in my mind.

- tireless footy player's legs meets sprinter's legs = sporting legend
- Mr Memory-for-Numbers meets Ms F-for-Maths = might just manage maths
- Elvis'n'Dylan fan meets Monteverdi'n'Mozart fan = eclectic music fan

- reading addict meets reading addict = reading hyper-addict
- big brown eyes meets hooded hazel eyes = big brown eyes (hopefully)
- pop singer meets opera singer = some kinda singer
- songwriter meets journalist = some kinda writer
- five foot nine meets five foot nine = five foot nine
- resigned father-of-three meets determined potential mother = besotted parents

This is what I remember most clearly. The hotel bathroom late one afternoon. The two of us lying together in the silky warm water of a deep bath. My back on his belly, his hands on my breasts. I am gently questioning him about how and where we will raise the child—if we have one. He has something else on his mind. The voice coming from behind my right ear is suddenly lawyer-like.

'And if we broke up?' He pauses. 'Would we have equal access to the child?'

I speak without thinking. 'I don't know. How could I bear to keep seeing you if we weren't together?'

Silence. He's so still. The tap at the other end of the bath begins to drip. The water has gone cold. I haven't noticed until now. I turn awkwardly, sloshing water over the side, and kiss his too-still face. He kisses me back, but absently, as if he's counting the drips.

reverence

IT'S 2018 and, after viewing the film footage of our father, my sister has been trawling the internet, searching for mentions of Glen. She's come across a blog written by the mother of one of the young musicians he saved from the wild surf before he drowned. There's a post about her daughter who 'always seems to fall on her feet'. The mother describes a series of 'scrapes' her daughter has been in over the course of her adult life—lucky escapes, near misses, fortunate coincidences. One of the stories the mother tells is about the time her daughter almost drowned at a surf beach. The tone is cheerful, lighthearted, proud. There's no mention of the loss of life that ensued—at least, not until a tiny footnote at the end of the post which mentions the 'unfortunate outcome'.

It's the same event, same true story, but it's like looking at yourself upside down in a mirror. Everything is real, but also wrong. And what about this story, the one I'm telling now about my quest to have a child? Does it seem upside down or inside out to others who were involved? The problem with true stories is that there are too many different truths. Perhaps this story would be more truthful if it was told as a conversation between me and the others involved. Or between me and my different 'selves'.

A few years ago, I came across some psychological theory about 'the dialogical self'. An Australian psychologist called Peter Raggatt has written about dialogical selves in storytelling. He asks, 'Can one's life be captured in a single, grand, synthesising story?' Trying to tell your life story, Raggatt says, assumes there is a 'linear, integrated and coherent tale to be told, with all the facts neatly tied together with a golden thread, a single narrative voice'. But the story you tell will be just 'one story from a number of possibilities, and therefore the life story could never be encompassed by a monologue. The life story is really more like a conversation of narrators, or perhaps a war of historians in your head.'

What would those warring historians say about my quest to become a mother?

— *Why did you want a child so badly?*
— Well…babies are adorable.
— *Oh, for heaven's sake. You can do better than that. What does adorable even mean? Do you mean like an Anne Geddes photograph? Or the Adoration of the Magi? Did you want a child to worship?*

- No, not to worship. To hold. I wanted another living thing to hold close to me. To be dependent on me. I wanted to care for someone other than myself. When I pictured myself as a mother, I always imagined myself doing things *for* the child. Feeding, bathing, smiling, reading, singing, teaching, protecting, soothing, consoling, loving the child. I'm not sure I ever pictured myself letting go of a grown child, though. Never got that far ahead in my fantasies.
- *Did you want a child who would worship you?*
- I want to say no. But I think the answer is yes. Someone who would love me as fiercely as I have loved my mother.
- *Perhaps you idealised the past, and the possible future. Did you ever think about the downsides of having a child?*
- Yes. I knew about the bad things that could happen to new mothers. The prolapses, the incontinence, the mastitis, the cystitis, the postnatal depression. I knew about Sudden Infant Death Syndrome. About mothers driven to infanticide. Watching other parents, I saw the tedium of parenting in their eyes. The hours and days and years spent wiping sticky faces and washing dirty clothes and managing filthy tantrums. Worrying about whether you can earn enough money to care for them. Worrying about their safety, monitoring their screen time, waiting for them to come home late at night. The shame of never being a perfect parent. I was aware of all the ways it's possible to lose a child—through silence, or sadness, or violence, or suicide, or geography, or illness, or ideology or religion. And I hated the infantilised gendered language of child rearing. Tots and bubs, nippers and moppets, mummies and daddies and kiddies. The weird sexist idioms like

120

yummy mummies and MILFs. (Have you noticed how these terms assume that most mothers are *not* sexually attractive—that the MILFs are the exception rather than the rule?) But none of that made a dent in the fantasy of hugging a child close, smelling their hair, studying the colour of their eyes. The human bond with them. Their physical presence.

— *Did you think having a child would give you a chance to 'do over' your own infancy? Give your child the attention, the attachment, the adoration you may have lost after your father drowned?*

— I don't know. It's a good theory. I've been wondering—can limerence apply to someone who doesn't exist? Was I in love—or 'in limerence'—with my imaginary child?

divergence

EARLY IN 2003, not long after Tom and I return from our Manly holiday, he has an afternoon gig at a local festival. The venue is a couple of blocks from my place, so we make a plan that he'll come over for a late-afternoon drink when he's done. Five o'clock comes and goes, then six o'clock. He's not responding to my text messages. Has something happened to him, or to one of the kids? Surely I would've heard by now. I try ringing him, but my calls go to voicemail.

By seven-thirty I'm a couple of glasses into the bottle of wine I'd been chilling for the two of us. Is this what it will be like if we have a child together and he has days when he doesn't feel like being 'tied down'? Will he ignore me and the child until he's ready to reappear? I pace between the living room and the back door, checking the outside stairwell in case he's about to knock.

Around nine o'clock there is a gentle tapping. I wrench open the door and stare at him. He's had a few glasses, too; I can smell them. He looks sheepish and knows not to try to kiss me. Turning on my heel I stride back into the living room, sit down on the couch and cross my arms.

'What's the matter?' he asks, standing in front of me.

'What happened to you?'

'Nothing happened, I just went out for a drink with an old friend. My battery was low so I turned the phone off.'

I stare at the floorboards, feeling sick. And then it comes.

'Sian, I need to talk to you.' He perches on the edge of the couch. 'Been thinking some more about the IVF thing.'

I want to stop time. I want to run out the back door and down the stairs and keep running until I reach the beginning of this strange day and rejoin time, perhaps around dawn, and know then that this is going to happen, and spend the long hours preparing myself for this conversation. Girding my heart.

'I've changed my mind,' he says. 'I don't want to do it.'

It's out now, and of course he doesn't want to. He never really wanted to, because I am not Cinderella and there is no such thing as happily ever after. Not in a story like this. There are more words spoken, some mine, some his, but they don't really matter. He tries to take my hand, but I pull away and jam my rigid body against the far end of the couch. When he says he hopes we can go back to 'the way we were', I shake my head. This is the end. There will be no father. The father has vanished. I will have to do this alone.

Fifteen years later, I'm teaching a university writing course. Each week the students read a different personal essay from an anthology, and we talk about the stories behind the situations described in these essays. We talk about how flawed memory is, and about how the memories we carry around with us are in part generated by our imaginations. 'We recreate memories like a jigsaw puzzle,' I explain, 'rather than literally recall them instant by instant. If someone tells you a relationship is over, for example, you will probably never forget that moment. But the details of what you remember happening after those words were spoken might not be entirely accurate.'

Everything leading up to Tom's announcement that night is still vivid to me, but what happened after I told him it was over? Did he linger, trying to dissuade me? Or did he walk out the back door, leaving me hunched on the couch? I have very few visual images, but I do have a physical imprint of the pain; my body remembers the clenching guts, the shrinking lungs, the racing heart. I couldn't stand up straight, had to bend a little to hold everything in.

Sometime in the next few days I must have made contact with the IVF counsellor, because I know there was another meeting. I retain a sense memory of trying to sit to attention while we spoke, trying to sound reconciled to Tom's latest decision—and our break-up—and explaining my intention to return to Plan A, using donor sperm. I can still feel the tightness in my face as I forced myself to smile at her.

There's also a memory fragment from a couple of weeks after that meeting, of stepping off a bus with a scouring pain under my ribs, knowing there was nothing physically wrong with me, but thinking this heart pain might kill me. Standing frozen at the bus stop I knew I had to give in, because I couldn't give Tom up. Not yet. There must have been some text messages, and a reunion, and I guess there was sex. There would have been relief from some of the pain, but there must also have been a settling of understanding about my place in his life. A settling for that place, in place of nothingness.

—

Back in our creative writing class, the students are reading an essay by an American writer about a girl who sees three teenagers nearly drown in a flooded river. At the back of the classroom a young man puts up his hand. 'Sian, was this a deliberate choice, the theme of all these essays?'

I'm baffled. 'What do you mean?'

'I mean, all the stories you've given us to read in this course have been about drownings or about the disappearance of a husband or a father.' The students are all staring at me, and some are nodding. They know about my father's death because I'd mentioned it in our first class. Now they've seen something that was invisible to me, the mind's secret work, the stirring and sifting and sorting, all going on behind my back. Once it's been pointed out, it's obvious. What else has my brain been keeping from me?

At home that night I open a computer file containing all the short stories I've ever written.

There's one about a young man who's befriended by a woman whose husband has suddenly died.

There's one about a middle-aged woman whose son has recently died.

There's one about a teenage girl who is suicidal, in which the narrator—a childless middle-aged woman—is trying to find the girl's parents.

There's one about a child called Sisyphus who has a giant boulder connected to him by an umbilical cord.

There's one about a woman who fantasises about murdering her husband.

There's one about a woman who, after her husband dies, tries to sell her children.

Parents, husbands, wives, children, death, again and again they surface in these stories, again and again there is trauma, crisis, fear, loss. Fictional exorcisms of a true story fifty years old.

bioscience

I WAS NEVER GOOD at science. In high school I memorised the table of elements because it sounded like a poem to me—*hydrogen, helium, lithium, beryllium*—but never understood how the elements fitted together. Even biology was hard. How cells behaved, how anatomical parts interacted, how genes transmitted information: none of this information would stick to my brain.

Twenty years after finishing high school, embarking on the IVF program feels like a return to this state of anxious ignorance. When the gynaecologist explains to me what will happen, she draws little pictures on a notepad to give me visual images of the process. An hour later I've forgotten the details. There will be lots of appointments and procedures, that much I gather. Appointments I can do. I keep a detailed diary, turn up for things on time. Remembering exactly what I'll be turning up for will be harder.

And there will be needles. Before the IVF specialists can start matchmaking my eggs with the donor sperm, they need to make sure I have a good supply of healthy ones. My egg production will be boosted with hormone injections, and it will be up to me to self-inject the magic fluids. I'm given a miniature suitcase containing vials of pharmaceuticals and plastic-wrapped syringes and told to make sure the drugs are refrigerated.

The first time I inject myself in the belly my hands are shaking. *Will it hurt? Have I got the right spot? What if there's an air bubble in the hypodermic?* Air bubbles are dangerous, I know that much, and I spend a long time studying the syringe to make sure it doesn't look like a spirit level. Then I pinch my belly skin and push the needle into the soft flesh. There's a slight delay before the sting, as if the nerves have been taking a nap and need to be woken up before they can register a protest. When the pain comes, it's surprisingly mild. Nothing like my memories of childhood vaccinations. Nothing that warrants a consoling lollipop. My pain threshold has clearly skyrocketed over the past few years. After three miscarriages, a prolapsed disc and back surgery, needles are easy-peasy.

The side effects of the hormones are harder to endure. My belly is bloated, my head aches and I feel tired all the time. Worst are the impacts on my mood. I've always suffered from PMT, becoming teary and anxious each month before I bleed. The hormones I'm taking seem to double the dread.

Perhaps this is why Tom is ignoring the whole IVF process. Have I become difficult, or not as entertaining as I used to be? Or is he simply not interested, now that he's not physically involved? Sometimes I wish he would offer to drive me to a medical appointment or pick me up from the hospital after a procedure. Make me a cup of tea and let me weep on his shoulder. Or even just ask how it's all going.

In his absence, my mother steps into the breach. Month after month she picks me up from the appointments, takes me to a café and hands me tissues as I ride the waves of hope and fear that accompany each egg-harvesting procedure, each embryo implant. The news from my gynaecologist is not good. I'm producing fewer eggs than they'd like, and those I do produce are not in great shape. A couple of times the fertilised embryo manages to cling to my uterus for a few days after my period is due, and I hold my breath, willing it to hang in there. I try not to move too suddenly in case I dislodge it—even though I know this is ridiculous. But then the bleeding begins again, and the whole complicated round of interventions has been in vain.

It all feels horribly familiar. No wonder Jack and I drifted apart. If at first you don't succeed, fail, fail, fail again.

Meanwhile my freelance work rolls on. I try to distract myself by focusing on my stories and reviews for the newspapers, and the new songs I'm learning. I've recently relinquished my position on the council of the Australian Conservation Foundation. On top of the gruelling IVF experience, the relentless bad news about species extinction and climate change has become unendurable. My brain has simply given up trying to assimilate the grim statistics of slow-motion ecocide.

I'm on a bunch of arts boards and committees and there's always an agenda to look at, a meeting to attend, grants to be awarded. Unlike climate science, the arts make me feel optimistic about humanity. And I'm determined to hang on to as much of my professional life as possible, in case the IVF doesn't work. But much of this activity is unpaid, and as the IVF bills flood in, the savings in my bank account slowly drain away. There's a limit to how long I can keep doing this, both financially and emotionally. I plough on. I'll be thirty-nine soon. This could be my last chance.

Tom still takes up a lot of my brain space. We're now spending every night together, either at my place or at his. I can't join him when he's away with the band anymore, because of the IVF schedule, but we manage a short holiday on the Queensland coast in the middle of the year. I'm so relieved to be away from Melbourne's winter, even the hormone injections are more bearable. When it's just the two of us, without family or work claiming his attention, I can staunch the trickle of resentment about him bailing out of IVF.

The coastal village where we're staying is only a few kilometres from the beach where my father drowned nearly four decades ago. Waking one morning in the early hours, listening to Tom's even breaths, I find myself wondering what my father's breathing sounded like when he slept.

There's so much I don't know about him. Did he dream of concert halls filled with applause? Did he wake in the night, as I often do, to wonder and worry?

If I do manage to have a child with the help of the anonymous sperm donor, what questions might my child have when they realise there is no flesh-and-blood father in their life? Will they feel that something is missing, a physical presence or a mirror image? What right do I have to deny my child half their genetic inheritance? I tell myself that I haven't suffered from the absence of a biological father. My stepfather John, the only father I've really known, is a kind, loyal, loving man whom I adore. Perhaps Tom will prove to be the same kind of stepfather, despite his misgivings.

—

Back in Melbourne, the IVF process grinds on. In November my gynaecologist tells me I have one stored embryo left. She's going on extended holidays over Christmas so if the next implant doesn't stick, we'll have to put things on hold for a few months. We're both baffled by my failure to produce good eggs. Could I have a mysterious condition that hasn't yet been diagnosed? Is this why I make such substandard eggs, and why I had three miscarriages? She can't give me an answer.

I don't know if I can keep going with this. Keep duelling with hope, month after month, picking myself back up every time. It's been seven years since I first started trying to have a child, nearly a fifth of my life. I've been looking at the statistics on childbirth. Last year, in 2002, there were two hundred and fifty thousand babies born in Australia, and four million babies born around the globe. There are babies everywhere, being pushed in prams along the streets of my suburb, being spoonfed in highchairs in my local café, smiling at me from posters on the sides of buses, bouncing up and down on television ads for toilet paper, being dandled above the shallows at my local beach. So many births, so many babies, and none of them mine.

The last embryo doesn't stick. I call my mother, and we meet at a café near her work. Sitting in an alcove away from the other customers, I weep into a paper napkin.

'I'm so tired,' I tell her. 'I want to get away. But when I try to work out what I want to get away from, I realise—it's me.' My mother is silent, at a loss. She can listen to me, hold my hand, but there is nothing she can do to fix this.

'I need to stop now.' As I hear myself speaking, I realise the decision has been made. The part-of-me-I-want-to-get-away-from has had enough. It's time to give up on the happy ending. Time to find out who I might be, if I'm not to be a mother.

silence

LIFE WAS QUIET in the Melbourne bayside suburb where I grew up. There was a golf course across the road from our house, screened behind tea-trees and wire fences. On weekends you could hear the regular *thwock* of golf clubs hitting balls. Every now and then one would come hurtling from the sky and land in our front yard, but even more exciting were the rare occasions when we got to spend our pocket money at the Mr Whippy van. Years later a friend of mine described how, when she was a child, her father told her that if the Mr Whippy music was playing it meant there was no ice-cream left. Adults lied—who knew?

There were few dramas and no tragedies in our neighbourhood, or none that reached the ears of children. There was the occasional bike stack when one of the boys next door came down the hill too fast on his Dragstar. There was the time I stood on a pitchfork in the front yard and my brother had to pull the prongs out of my bleeding foot, but nothing a bandage and a tetanus injection couldn't fix.

Then one night, when I was eleven years old, a girl in our suburb disappeared from her bedroom. She was a couple of years younger than me, but superficially we looked alike. Same blonde hair, blunt fringe and toothy smile staring at me from the front page of my parents' newspaper. She had gone to bed at the usual time, and when her mother woke the next morning the girl was no longer there. The morning after that, she was a news story. People can disappear without notice. This is what I learned that day. Relearned.

Why did it matter to me that she and I looked alike? Perhaps it made it easier to imagine someone grabbing *my* blonde hair and dragging me out the window into the dark night. I replayed that scene over and over in the weeks following her disappearance, lying awake in the bedroom my brother and I shared, wishing he would stay awake and talk to me and ward off the shadow-man I imagined was lurking outside the window.

Not long after that girl disappeared in my childhood suburb, police officers knocked on our front door. They were conducting a house-to-house search and wanted to look around our garden. My brother and I had been digging roads for his toy cars in the backyard so there was freshly turned earth. As the police poked around in the dirt, I felt guilty, as if I was hiding something from them.

They left, and weeks and months and years passed and

still the police found nothing. The children in our street stopped talking about the missing girl and went back to picking up stray golf balls. The girl faded from my memory, but three decades after her disappearance her mother was on the television again. Her pain hadn't lessened. It was in her voice as she repeated two words over and over into the waiting microphones—'a mystery, a mystery, a mystery'.

—

In the 1970s, when a white Australian child was kidnapped from her home, there was a massive police hunt, weeks of media coverage and the offer of a huge reward. There was public outrage, and an outpouring of compassion towards her devastated family.

Compassion has always had well-defined limits in this country. From the beginning of the twentieth century up until the 1970s, tens of thousands of Aboriginal and Torres Strait Islander children were kidnapped from their homes. These weren't random acts of unforeseen evil. These kidnappings were part of a so-called assimilation policy orchestrated and conducted by the Australian government.

Two decades ago Indigenous footballer and anti-racism campaigner Michael Long described his mother's kidnapping in a letter to a newspaper editor:

> Does (Prime Minister) Howard understand how much trauma my grandmother suffered? It ripped her heart out, what she went through. Back then my mother had no choice but to go. It was wrong.

> My mother was taken when she was a baby, taken
> to Darwin and put on a boat—she had never seen
> the sea before—screaming and yelling, not knowing
> what was happening and then crying herself to sleep.
> I am so angry anyone could do this to a child just
> because their skin was a different colour. My mother
> has been dead for 17 years. Who is going to tell her
> story, the trauma and lies associated with her people
> and their families? (*Age,* 5 April 2000)

Some powerful white men thought the government should go further than mere kidnapping. In 1984 one of the wealthiest men in Australia, mining magnate Lang Hancock, was interviewed on national television about his views on 'the Aboriginal problem'. Dressed in the clean white shirt favoured by white male businessmen of the time, Hancock told the white male interviewer,

> The ones that are no good to themselves, that can't
> accept things, the half-castes—and this is where
> most of the trouble comes from—I would dope the
> water up so that they were sterile and would breed
> themselves out in the future and that would solve
> the problem.

After his death in 1995, Lang Hancock was described in his *Canberra Times* obituary as a 'pioneer and a visionary'.

It took until 2007 for the Australian government to publicly acknowledge the crimes committed against members of the Stolen Generations. Even as Prime Minister Kevin Rudd was issuing a formal apology on behalf of the government, some conservative members of parliament walked out in protest.

In this country the lives of some people's children have always been valued more highly than the lives of other people's children. The stories of those other people's children are not mine to tell. All I can say is *sorry—sorry—sorry—sorry—sorry—*

perseverance

IT'S LATE 2004 and I am remaking myself—or perhaps, unmaking the part of me that was going to be a mother. I'm doing everything all at once—writing newspaper articles, singing in concerts, making radio documentaries, and reviving precious friendships I neglected during the year of IVF. My environmental activism has shrunk to a few benefit concerts and newspaper opinion pieces. Climate scientists are warning that land temperatures this year have been the fourth hottest on record; ocean temperatures, the third hottest. Thinking about the future paralyses my ability to enjoy the present. I try to persuade myself there's no point worrying about it. By the time things get so bad that much of the planet is uninhabitable, I'll be dead. There will be no children or grandchildren of mine left to deal with the mess. The future promises only pain. The present, on the other hand, is full of pleasure.

Being involved with Tom's extended clan is like being on a giant cruise ship. There's always something going on—pub gigs featuring his sister's or one of his nephews' bands; dinners and conversations about art and politics with his brothers and their partners; his daughters' school concerts; plays directed by his second ex-wife. Exhibition openings, football matches, birthday parties, book launches, a never-ending round of social events. For a shy person it's exhausting, but exhilarating. I'm in love with this family and their company is consolation for knowing I will never create a family of my own.

I'm trying to spend more time with Tom's daughters, who are now ten and twelve, but my timing is off. Their mother has recently moved out of Melbourne, taking the girls with her. Their new schools and friendship networks are over an hour away from us, so they no longer spend every second week with their father. But there are still precious weekends and school holidays with trips to the pool, the beach; basketball hoop sessions and movie nights. I'm up for them all.

One day, as we're driving the girls back to their mother's place, the older one pipes up from the back seat. 'Sian, why do you laugh so much?'

Her question makes me laugh, of course. 'I must be happy,' I tell her. She beams at me in the rear-vision mirror and, right now, it feels as if this will be enough.

But I'm still feeling bone tired. One Saturday morning,

as the girls and I are chasing a basketball around an outdoor court, I become so breathless I have to lie down gasping on the concrete. How can I be so unfit? My diet is healthy, I exercise regularly. Is this the aftermath of IVF, my body letting me know about that year of interventions? I pick myself up and stagger back onto the court for another round.

The following year, 2005, I pack up my flat and move into Tom's house. Between us we have too much furniture and way too many books, but we cram it all in. It's quieter at his place these days: the girls want to spend their weekends hanging out with their friends. It's understandable, they're adolescents now, but I miss them. Tom and I try to keep an afternoon clear each week to head out of town and visit them. Their mother is invariably warm and welcoming, but I can never quite relax in her home. There is her stove, on which she cooks nourishing meals for *their* children. There is her fridge, from which *their* children help themselves to snacks. There is her bed, in which perhaps *their* children were conceived. A rogue inner voice whispers, *this is the last woman he wanted to have children with. Why her? Why not me?*

That voice. It can be shamefully petty. At the beach with the girls the following summer, I bridle when Tom suggests we divide the cost for the rented apartment between the two of us. *Wait a minute,* the voice argues, *why should I help pay for his children when he didn't want to be burdened with our child?*

I only succeed in muting half the message and it comes out as pure stinginess. 'I don't think I should have to pay for the girls, do you?' Tom is silent, his face expressionless.

It's not his fault I'm childless. Our timing was off. I have chosen this life. I'm the laughing stepmother, the adaptable girlfriend, the late-boarding passenger on the family cruise ship, seated at the captain's table every night. I cannot also be a petulant sulk. That voice must be silenced.

nonsense

IT'S WINTER 2016 and I'm driving to the coast again. My campervan is idling at the lights behind a dusty blue station wagon. On the left side of the station wagon's rear window is a sticker. One, two, three, four, five stick figures all in a row, from tallest to smallest, all smiling and holding hands. No words are necessary. We all know what this signifies— *My Family*. What is it *for*, though?

Stick figures are the international shorthand for a child's drawing so this is meant to be an adult's imagining of a child's imagining of their nuclear family, right? If so, why do adults need to render their family unit through the imaginary eyes of their children? And *who* is it for? Is it bragging? *Look, fellow drivers, at what my loins produced!*

Is it self-reassurance? *Thank god—I have achieved the thing I'm meant to achieve in my life: a standard family unit.*

Is it an advertisement of attachment and allegiance? *This is what matters most to me in the world.* My first two cars were covered in stickers, most of them bearing slogans for political causes I cared about. Tools of persuasion. But who is being persuaded by these stick figures, and of what?

Is it a protective device, stuck there in the expectation that if another driver knows you have a five-member family they will be less likely to plough into you? Or is it a status symbol, like a personalised numberplate?

A friend who used to live in Peru told me the government there had banned these stickers. They were wildly popular at the time, especially among the wealthy, but they were like inventory notes for kidnappers. Big expensive cars advertised the owners' wealth, and the sticker indicated how many children they had inside.

If I were to put a stick-figure sticker on the back of my van, what would it look like? Me on one side of the rear windscreen with a small unkempt dog at my feet, and far away on the other side, a cavalcade of stick figures signifying Tom's clan, each one covered with a big red X. We could also add three tiny foetuses—why not?

The lights change and I overtake the blue station wagon, sneaking a look inside. No children's car seats. No children. Just a middle-aged woman tapping her fingers rhythmically on the steering wheel. Is the sticker a relic of times past? Perhaps the husband left her. Perhaps the children grew up and left home. Perhaps they no longer speak to her because she left the husband. Or because they're in jail.

Now she's a middle-aged woman alone in her vehicle. Just like me.

'Stick-figure sticker fuckers,' I say out loud. Then I say it again, louder. It feels good.

grievance

IT'S 2007, and it's been nearly four years since I gave up on IVF. I'm teaching part-time in a university writing course. The classes start early in the evening and finish late, and I'm often so tired I can't wait to catch the train home and crawl into bed. At the beginning of second semester, I set aside an evening for one-on-one meetings with my students. By the end of the first hour of consultations I'm feeling light-headed and nauseous. I usher a student out of the room and shut the door behind her. Sitting down again, I rest my woozy head on the desk. The door opens and another student comes in.

'Can you just give me a few minutes?' I say, raising my head. 'Not feeling great.'

He sits down and opens a folder of work. 'I'm on time,' he says, 'this won't take long.' But something strange is happening to my vision. The punctual student is blurry. My head lowers itself to the desk.

'Jeez, Sian,' he says, paying attention now, 'you don't look crash hot.'

I raise my head again. 'Can you do me a favour, call a taxi?' He pulls out his phone and soon I am floating down the stairs and into the back of a cab, where I lie down on the pungent vinyl and close my eyes. A few seconds later, or so it feels, I'm outside our front gate, scrabbling in my bag for some cash. There's no one home, Tom's away again, so I dump my stuff, kick off my shoes and climb under the bedcovers fully clothed.

In the morning I still feel exhausted. I've recently found a new doctor and she offers to squeeze me in at the end of her long day, so late in the afternoon I drag myself to her surgery.

'I'm tired all the time,' I tell her. 'Have been for years. And it's getting worse.'

She asks about my diet and suggests an iron deficiency. Then I tell her about how hard it is for me to stay warm in winter, no matter how many layers I wear. And about my dry skin and slow digestive system and brittle fingernails. She chews on her pen, studying my pale face.

'A blood test will tell us about your iron levels, but we'll test for a few things. There might be something else going on.'

Something else? I can't bear to ask what she means. My body has sprung so many nasty surprises on me over the last decade.

A few days later I'm back in her office and she's staring at her screen. 'Your iron levels are definitely very low,' she says. 'You need to get yourself some iron tablets. But there's something else…Looks like hypothyroidism, from those TSH levels. You have a low-functioning thyroid. You'll need to take regular medication for that. It hasn't entirely stopped working, which is why you've been able to keep functioning. But the iron deficiency on top of the thyroid problem must have tipped you over the edge.'

I'm not even sure what my thyroid does. Back home I do an internet search. 'The thyroid gland secretes the hormones thyroxine and triiodothyronine.' I try saying that last word out loud, but it defeats me. 'Hypothyroidism occurs when the thyroid gland does not produce enough thyroid hormones. If hypothyroidism is not treated, the symptoms slowly get worse, and it becomes more and more difficult to function normally. Symptoms include tiredness, sore muscles, constipation and sensitivity to the cold.' I remember that morning on the basketball court with Tom's girls, how I'd been flattened by a short bout of exercise. How tired I've felt for over a decade. Then I read this: 'Also fertility problems and increased risk of miscarriage.'

Wait. What?

Is this it—finally? The answer to the mystery? Did I waste seven long years because of a dicky thyroid? All those people I consulted while trying to have a child—the medical specialists, the naturopaths, the Chinese herbalists—did *any* of them investigate the cause of my ongoing fatigue?

Should I try again? Sort out my thyroid and climb back on the IVF merry-go-round?

The thought only lasts a few seconds. I'm nearly forty-three years old. Even without the handicap of a thyroid problem, my chances of success would be sliver-slim.

It's too late.

—

A decade later I come across a newspaper article about a seventy-three-year-old Indian woman who's given birth to healthy twins via IVF. According to the reporter, the woman and her husband 'always wanted children but have been unable to conceive until now'.

Did I give up too soon?

On the day of their birth the twins' eighty-two-year-old father was asked who would care for the children if anything happened to him and his wife. 'Nothing is in our hands,' he replied. 'Whatever should happen will happen. It is all in the hands of God.' The day after that, the father had a stroke.

Should they have given up earlier?

I try to imagine myself into the mind of the twins' mother. The decades of hope and disappointment, the cruel optimism of her quest, and its dark sequel.

There's a book with the title *Cruel Optimism* by an American cultural theorist called Lauren Berlant. She uses the phrase to describe the unachievable fantasies of the good life that have proliferated in liberal democracies. Berlant argues that our attachments to the ingredients of this so-called good life—food, popular culture, love, family—are all optimistic. Each of these 'objects of desire' represents a cluster of promises that we want someone or something to make to us, and to make possible for us. The promises could be embedded in a thing, an institution, a text—or, she writes, 'a bunch of cells'.

Is my fantasy of a happy ending a fetish peculiar to privileged white people like me?

Sometimes, Berlant says, our attachment to these 'objects of desire' can be an obstacle to our flourishing. Cruel optimism is an attachment to something that is 'discovered to be impossible, sheer fantasy, or toxic'.

My impossible child. My toxic fantasy of lifelong love with Tom. In the end, these enduring attachments had caused me more pain than pleasure. But then, optimism runs in my family. Our attachments are long and strong, especially to the people we love. My grandmother Peg, for example: nothing could persuade her that the world and its people weren't on a continual path of improvement, an infinite renewal of love and kindness. Toxicity simply wasn't in her emotional range. Peg also loved babies—not just the four daughters she had, or the ten children her daughters had, but the babies with Down syndrome and cerebral palsy whom she nursed for many years in a children's home. Was her optimism fuelled by her attachment to all those babies?

Her eldest daughter, my mother Margot, must be an optimist at heart. Her work as a child psychologist has all been about trying to make life better for vulnerable children. Children on the autism spectrum. Children with dyslexia.

149

First Nations children whose families are crumbling with grief. She's chiselled away with her research tools, shaping new knowledge. She rarely speaks optimistically about the future, and often anticipates the worst. Perhaps, since my father's death, this has been her way of reminding herself about the inevitability—and the ordinariness—of suffering. But her intellectual impulses have always been hopeful.

'Cruel optimism,' writes Lauren Berlant, 'is the condition of maintaining an attachment to a problematic object *in advance of* its loss.' But Lauren, how was I to know that loss would be the only outcome of my quest to have a child? Through all those long years, I always believed I would become a mother. I understood the statistics, and that the IVF industry is by necessity a purveyor of cruel optimism. I thought I would be an exception.

—

Not long after the hypothyroidism diagnosis I call Jack, suggesting we meet. Since our relationship ended five years ago, we've stayed in touch, catching up three or four times a year for birthdays and Christmas. We share a meal and exchange extravagant gifts and news of friends and family. He knows about my year of IVF, but I've spared him the details.

He agrees to meet me for lunch in a café near his house. After the usual niceties, he tells me he's started 'seeing someone', a woman with a young son. He's been spending a lot of time with the child, kicking a footy, going to movies.

He looks happier than he has for a long time. Maybe I should let sleeping dogs lie. But my next sentence has already formed itself.

'I've just been diagnosed with a thyroid condition.'

Jack is immediately concerned for me. Is it serious? Am I okay?

'It's fine, the medication can sort it out. But this condition…it can cause miscarriages and fertility problems. So you weren't the problem. It was me.'

Is that relief on his face? Jack reaches over the table, takes my hands in his and squeezes them gently. Then he lets go.

dehiscence

ONE EVENING IN AUTUMN 2008 as we're finishing dinner, Tom receives a phone call from his son. As he listens, his face softens in a way I've never seen before. 'That's great news,' he says quietly. He's smiling broadly now. 'Is it public yet?'

His son's girlfriend takes over on the other end of the line and Tom's voice becomes so very tender. When the conversation ends he stands there, staring down at the phone. He shakes his head, chuckles and finally looks up at me. 'They're having a baby.'

A tightening in my gut. Then my head takes over and manages to activate the appropriate facial muscles. 'Wow— that's big news! Congratulations, Grandad.'

My face isn't right yet. 'How do you feel?' I ask, buying time.

As he speaks there is a ferocious skirmish going on just behind my eyes.

This is good news.

This is painful news. News I craved, so often, for myself.

But mostly it's good news. For fuck's sake, smile.

At last, I'm making the right face and standing up from the dinner table so I can hug the grandfather-to-be. Something is still lurking.

—

It's late spring 2008 and Tom and I are walking through the city holding hands, on our way to see a play. There's an arts festival in full swing and the streets are buzzing with people. We're talking about the visiting theatre company when I see that same tender smile spreading over his face. He lets go of my hand and holds his arms out in front of him as if waiting for a hug. I turn to see his son's girlfriend approaching us, all belly and blushes, opening her arms wide too. They embrace. 'You look so beautiful!' he tells her.

It's not just hurt I'm wrangling. It's also anger, and hot shame, the three emotions crawling around behind my squinting eyes.

Later that night, inside my head, I'm explaining to Tom why it's hard for me to see him so happy about his daughter-in-law's pregnancy; to hear him praising her beauty as she strolls down the street with his grandchild inside her; how I can't help thinking about how he didn't want to stroll down the street with me carrying his child. But I say nothing.

It's December 2008 and we've driven down the coast for a weekend at the beach. Soon after we arrive there's a phone call—*it's a boy!*—and we open a bottle of champagne to toast the first grandson, Jay. I drink too much, trying to loosen the tight ache under my ribs.

The next day we hike to a lookout with an endless view over the coastline. I search in vain for the horizon, camouflaged behind sea mist, and suck in the gusting southerly wind, but the tightness remains. The gap between how I feel and how I'm meant to be feeling yawns wider and wider.

Tom is itching to return home, so late on Sunday morning we drive back down the highway. After dropping me off, he hurries to the hospital, disappointed that I've chosen not to go with him. I thought I might feel better alone, away from his joy, but soon I'm pacing the hallway, whimpering. *What is the matter with me?*

An hour later I'm curled up on the bed, hyperventilating, overwhelmed by an urge to escape this house, this body, this mind. *Where to go?* I open the laptop and search online for motels. A place pops up just a couple of kilometres away and there's a room available. I throw some clothes into a bag and drive down the road to a small hotel. The receptionist pretends not to notice my tear-swollen eyes, quickly handing me a key and pointing me towards the stairs.

The room is almost entirely taken up by a king-sized bed. With the door locked behind me, the only sound I can hear is the low hum of an invisible fridge. I curl up on the vast mattress, waiting to feel safe. Instead, the whimpering begins again. *I need Tom. Why doesn't he come for me?* There's no logic to this: he thinks I'm at home. He's with the first-born child of the next generation. He's immersed in the joys of begetting, nursing a blanket-wrapped morsel of life that would not exist if not for him. He can feel his grandson's tiny heart: he made a family, and now they have begun making their own families, and there's no end in sight to this process of making and making again.

I am lying on a king-sized raft in the middle of a silent, roiling ocean and striding towards me through the noiseless white-tops is a giant clutching a drowned man in one fist and three dead foetuses in the other. The giant is muttering *fee fi fo fum, fee fi fo fum* and at last this liquid terror of mine has a name.

It's grief.

nurturance

A DECADE AFTER that night in the hotel I'm listening to a woman on the radio talking about miscarriages. She's on a campaign to have *this disenfranchised grief,* as she calls it, publicly acknowledged. The silence around a miscarriage can be 'isolating and invalidating', she says. Grief is always based on connection, and for women who lose a wanted pregnancy, the grief is about the loss of connection to their unborn child, the loss of their 'hopes and dreams and fantasies'. For some women, miscarriages can cause post-traumatic stress disorder.

When the interview ends, I go to the computer and do a search for PTSD. I click a link and find this description of symptoms: *The person relives the event through unwanted and recurring memories, often in the form of vivid images and night-mares. There may be intense emotional or physical reactions, such as sweating, heart palpitations or panic when reminded of the event.*

Sufferers often experience 'anger, guilt and shame' and feel 'cut off from others'. PTSD can also affect how you remember events, chewing holes in your memories.

There are gaps in my memory of that night in the hotel after Jay was born. Did I fall asleep? Did I think about sleeping forever? Did I wake in the morning and realise that no one was coming to find me, and no one else could banish the red-headed giant? Did I drive meekly home and wait for Tom's irritation with me to pass? I don't know. Something fierce has scoured those memories away.

~

The story recommences with love. Tom and I become keen babysitters—the paternal grandfather and the de facto stepgrandmother. As often as we can, we drive to Tom's son's home on the other side of town to feed Jay his mushy dinners, change his mushy nappies and put him to bed with stories and music. As he learns to speak, Jay says my name often. Every time he does, it's a precious gift.

When Jay reaches his second year, we acquire a portable cot and sometimes he stays overnight with us. He's an easygoing child, happy to be lowered into the bathtub, happy to push a plastic boat from one end to the other, happy to blow water through the snorkel we find in the girls' toybox, happy to be lifted out of the bathtub, towelled dry and eased into his pyjamas. I buy him a book about tractors and diggers, and he sits with me on the couch, pointing out his favourites and making the noises the diggers make in his imagination. He wants to know the name of everything in the world, and loves to list those names—tractors, Lego pieces, birds, dogs, playground equipment—so many different names for so many things. He wants to mow the back lawn with me, so I let him push our little electric mower around the garden—unplugged. Quite often his sentences start with, 'Sian, did you know...?' and even if I did know, I feign ignorance and wait for him to tell me about his latest discovery.

In the second summer of his life Jay's parents take him to visit his maternal grandparents, who live in Perth. Tom and I—and the two girls—are also invited. We'll all be holidaying together in a beach house on the south coast of Western Australia. It's a new variation on this sprawling, multi-generational blended family, but the pleasures are the same—the company of vivid minds, long conversations about art, science and politics—with the addition of goofy after-dinner games with the kids. The days are hot and dry, and Jay has his first taste of those bleached Indian Ocean beaches. He potters in the shallows, picking up shells and poking his fingers inside them. We show him a giant red rock that looks like an elephant and who knows, maybe it once was, or soon will be. Seen through Jay's eyes, even the most improbable transformations seem possible.

But something is still lurking out there, beyond the breakers. It's hard to quash my envy when I notice the physical similarities between Jay and his grandmother. Same cheekbones, same long-lashed eyes. The girls, now in their mid-teens, have become reluctant to sit with us on the beach. They prefer to lie at a distance, on their towels, looking out for boys who might be looking out for them. I miss their company, but I recall the same scene playing out on the beaches of my adolescence, when sitting with my parents felt like an admission of failure.

One hot night, lying beside Tom under a circling fan, I find myself weeping. He's baffled by my tears—again—as I sink under the waves. Soon my wrenching sobs are being blown around the bedroom by the ceiling fan, and I worry that the sound might wake everyone in the beach house, but I can't stop. Comforting others is not Tom's forte. He lies rigid beside me, waiting for the noises to go away. In this moment we are as far apart as the opposite coasts of this wide dry continent.

⌒

It's 2019 and I've been reading an article about tears. In 'Weeping and Transformations of the Self', Australian sociologist Jack Barbalet says that when a transformation of self is expansive, tears of joy express it. When it is negative or depletive, he writes, it is 'expressed by tears of sadness. *I do not weep because I am cold. I weep because I am cold when I am used to being—or expect to be—warm.*'

I remember my midnight tears in that West Australian beach house, and how impossible it was to explain where the misery came from. We had just spent a sunny day at the beach, surrounded by people we loved. We had put the tricky issue of our possible child behind us. We were healthy, safe and still together. Why was it that I felt so bereft?

Weeping, Professor Barbalet writes, can help to 'harmonise or reintegrate a person's self-concept after events that have disrupted a prior self-image and self-feelings'. For four decades my self-image was of someone who would one day have a baby. *I weep because I am childless when I expected to be a mother.* My tears were more than sadness. They were a physical expression of that absence.

'What is discharged in weeping,' Barbalet says, 'is an image of self that is not tolerable. Weeping is expression of emotional meanings in place of…speech.' Tom and I were good with words: we both earned a living that way. Why were we so inarticulate back then? I was embarrassed by the childish voice in my head still yelling how unfair it was; ashamed of my residual anger with all the people who'd got what I wanted. My childless self was intolerable to me.

Professor Barbalet also writes about self-pity, which he describes as 'an emotional apprehension of failure to attain an expected condition or opportunity'. I'd expected to be a parent, and those expectations were dashed. *What to expect when you're not expecting.* But not everyone who fails to get what they want becomes stuck, wallowing. Some use their failure as a spur to success in other areas. The failed screenwriter who writes a best-selling novel. The failed politician who becomes a captain of industry, telling the politicians what to do. Was my failure to overcome failure another form of failure?

Barbalet says self-pity 'includes a perception of one's own impotence'. Even though I had tried hard to assert control over my situation—finding a sperm donor, doing solo IVF for a year—in the end I was powerless in the face of my body's intransigence. And afterwards I doggedly pushed on, telling myself it was all 'behind me'—afraid of my lingering grief. *The things we fear usually catch up with us.* Is this what my mother did, too, after her husband drowned—tried to outrun misery?

I keep digging. Reading a journal article by an English sociologist called Susie Scott, the keywords resonate with me: *absence, emptiness, invisibility, silence, nothing*. She writes about what she calls 'a sociology of nothing'. I can picture the right-wing shock jocks barking like affronted seals: 'Your tax dollars at work—boffins paid to think about nothing!'

But maybe Susie Scott is onto something. She proposes a distinction between the words nothing and nothingness. '*Nothingness* (is) the *absence of something*,' she writes, but '*nothing* (is) the *absence of everything*.'

In our culture, private griefs often remain invisible. We mark our grand communal griefs with bronze statues and public holidays, with speeches full of comforting platitudes. But a private grief is hidden, an empty well. We long for that emptiness to be filled, for absence to be replaced with presence, for *nothing* to become *something*. Or to be acknowledged as being *something*.

It's important, writes Susie Scott, to 'understand the unmarked'. Like an early miscarriage? I remember the second one, and the medico with the ultrasound wand who stared at her screen and said, 'There's nothing there. Are you sure you were pregnant?' I remember the non-presence of those precious cell clusters, the emptiness, the silence between Jack and me when we drove home from the hospital. We had no rituals to mark those losses. No coffins, no graves, no laments. No words to fill the growing gulf between us.

The ultrasound magician was wrong. She should have said 'there's *nothingness* there', because, yes, I *had* been pregnant. There had been the potential for a lifetime of *something* growing inside me, and that something also had the potential to create other lives, generations of people, infinite possible combinations of fingers and toes, eyes and ears. Infinite tantrums and tendernesses. But back then, after the bleeding stopped, there was only absence.

⁓

Two-year-old Jay is sitting next to me on a couch, holding my right hand. He counts off my fingers, reciting the words I've taught him—'blue ring, pearl ring, silver ring'. He stops and smiles up at me.

'Correct!' I reply, offering him my left hand next.

'Green ring, purple ring, moo' ring!' he says, his voice rising in triumph.

'Yes, *mood* ring, you're right!'

He taps the mood ring with a gentle Morse code. This

one's his favourite, perhaps because the mood ring is also sometimes a blue ring, a green ring or a purple ring. Objects have names, names are also colours, colours can change, and isn't the world amazing?

This isn't limerence. It's something softer, easier. This is what I've wanted. To see the world again through the eyes of a child, to remember that sense of amazement, to relearn the lesson that, although there are rules, not everything in the world follows them, and that those exceptions can be the most amazing things of all. Moments like this, I tell myself, will have to be enough.

Sometimes, when Jay asks me a question I can't answer, I fudge and say, 'It's a mystery.' He repeats the word *mystery* over and over, as if the telling of it will unlock its secrets. Sometimes, when he's crouching over a dead moth or an interesting pebble, I hear him whisper to himself: 'It's a mystery.'

I think he will be a scientist.

liquescence

A FRIEND RECENTLY sent me a list of words for things I didn't realise had names. The space between your eyebrows is the *glabella*. The wired cage that holds the cork in a bottle of champagne is an *agraffe*. Illegible handwriting is *griffonage*. The armhole in clothes, where the sleeves are sewn, is an *armscye*. And the cry of a newborn baby is called *vagitus*.

I never tallied up exactly how much money I paid to medical specialists over the years in pursuit of vagitus. Couldn't see the point. I spent what I had and tried for as long as I could bear. Then I stopped.

In pursuit of another kind of vagitus, I've also spent a lot of money on singing lessons. I began learning in my early twenties and continued until my late thirties. In that time my voice went from a breathy piping thing to a passable lyric soprano, and in part that's thanks to a technique called 'the baby cry'.

It's one of the most effective methods for developing a sound that can reach the back stalls of a concert hall. When you're a newborn baby your vocal technique is as perfect—and as loud—as it will ever be. Your tiny cords are in alignment and you haven't yet developed bad vocal habits. But it doesn't last. If you want a voice powerful enough to fill an opera house, you have to relearn how to sound utterly helpless.

'Say *nyah*,' my teacher said, 'putting the sound as far up your nasal passages as you can.'

'*Nyaaah!*' I snarled, but it was never as loud as my neighbours' newborn, whose cries cut through double-brick walls.

Eventually I abandoned the idea of becoming a fulltime opera singer. A passable voice is not enough, you need a glorious one, and that was always beyond me. So why did I spend all those years trying to sound like a helpless baby?

When I was a child some of my friends had dolls that cried like a newborn if you pressed a button on their stomachs. I didn't need one. I had an invisible button of my own. That sense of helplessness lay just under the surface, and it didn't take much to set me off.

My family grew weary of my frequent tears. 'Stop that moaning,' they scolded, but I didn't know how. The tears came from somewhere or something out of my control, something inchoate, pre-verbal, something so desolate it couldn't be named. Something that began half a century ago on a windy surf beach, perhaps, where something was lost so suddenly I've felt winded ever since.

dissonance

IT'S 2011 and Tom has been away for months, touring with his band. We used to have, as a way of enduring these separations, a ritual involving a plastic heart-shaped token that popped out of a Christmas cracker a few years ago. It was red and had the words 'I love you' painted on it, and every time he went away for work, I'd stash it somewhere in his luggage—a game of hide and seek, with a love heart standing in for a lover. I'd wait like a child for him to discover it stuffed inside a sock or between the pages of a novel and send me a triumphant text message. When he came home, he'd hide the heart somewhere in the house for me to find—inside a pillowcase, perhaps, or in the cupboard under the kitchen sink.

Sometime in the past year, the love heart went missing while he was away. Maybe I hid it too cleverly. Maybe he took the sock containing the little red heart to a laundromat, and it's still clattering around inside a washing machine somewhere on the other side of the world. Or maybe, after ten years together, he's tired of the game. I try not to dwell on it.

When he comes home at the end of this latest tour, he's even quieter than usual. He's been working hard for a long time. Maybe it's exhaustion. Even the birth of his second grandson, Jay's younger brother, doesn't bring us closer. Maybe he's nervous, after what happened when Jay was born. Maybe he thinks I'm going to start crying again. This time, though, I'm unreservedly happy about the new baby. Someone else for me to love.

One day in October, I find myself sitting on the kitchen floor, scrubbing away at the cupboard under the kitchen sink like a madwoman. Trying to make everything around me as perfect as it was ten years ago when we first got together.

Late that night Tom and I have a conversation in our bedroom in which he finally explains his silences. There is a sensation of falling, as if a stage floor has collapsed. Our conversation lasts about three minutes, the same length as an average pop song.

⁓

Eight years later I'm standing in the middle of a crowd at an inner-city pub, watching an album launch. Three women wend their way onstage through a thicket of mic stands and find their places. They take a deep breath in unison and the music begins. I'm listening intently, trying to decipher the lyrics of these harmony-saturated songs, stories of loves lost and found, affirmations for vulnerable hearts, celebrations of survival. Then, about halfway through the set, the singer who invited me here leans into her microphone and announces, 'This one's called "More Women".'

The song is about a woman whose man is leaving her. He had recently told her not to worry, that he was faithful. Now he's changed his mind. She's not enough for him. He says he needs 'more women'.

More women, the three singers croon sweetly. Now some in the crowd are singing along softly, *more women,* and as more and more fans join in and the sound swells around me, I fade into the night.

ascendance

HOW HEAVY is grief? Heavier than a sleepy toddler being lifted out of a cot. Heavier than the slumped body of a post-coital lover or a drowned man.

It's December 2011, two months after the break-up, and I'm back living with my sister. Every morning when I wake it takes a few moments for me to remember what has happened to my life, and when I do, my heart begins racing to the end of another impossibly long day. Part of me is still waiting for Tom to change his mind, admit he made a mistake, invite me to come home again. Another part knows how fantastical this is. The last time he changed his mind about anything was when he pulled out of IVF, eight years ago. He doesn't vacillate. It's over.

The Christmas holidays loom ahead like an impassable mountain range. Yoni and her family are going camping with a huge group of friends and they've invited me along, but I can't bear the thought of trying to be sociable with dozens of strangers. Then my old friend Nella calls with an invitation. Would I like to go bushwalking with her and her partner Andrew over the New Year break? As soon as she mentions the Snowy Mountains, I know this is exactly what I need. A chance to stare at a far horizon, suck in some thinner air. Conquer the emotional vertigo that has gripped me for the last two months.

The day after Boxing Day, Nella and Andrew pick me up and we drive east through Gippsland. In the town of Bairnsdale we stop for fuel and chocolate. Out the front of the petrol station a giant inflatable tube figure is waving madly at passing cars, trying to attract customers. As I wait in the back of the car for Nella to get the petrol, the air supply to the waving man is abruptly switched off. He collapses slowly onto the pavement like he's been king-hit from behind, but in slow motion, and I think: I know how you feel.

On Christmas Day Yoni gave me a plastic inflatable Santa. She's the keeper of quirky family traditions, and she remembered that as a child I loved these blow-up toys. The new Santa has a weighted base: if you try to push it over, it bounces straight back up again. Maybe there's a message there.

Tank full, Nella, Andrew and I drive north over the border to the southern New South Wales town of Jindabyne. I shade my eyes against the glare of the sun reflecting off the lake that zigzags past the town. A lone windsurfer tracks across the water, abruptly tips over and disappears from view.

He soon re-emerges, shaking his head, and I long to join him in that icy reservoir, to feel the shock of it in my bones.

West of the town, along the Alpine Way, we pull up at a guesthouse in the foothills of Mount Crackenback. 'Great location for a chiropractic conference,' Andrew says, smiling at me from the rear-vision mirror. It's funny, and my mouth tries to make the right shape in response. The guesthouse is eccentric. There's a main lodge and a rambling collection of cottages, all set in landscaped gardens dotted with sculptures. We pass an open shed with a dusty upright piano abandoned to the elements. Poor piano.

While Nella and Andrew settle into their cottage, I lug my bags to the main lodge. I've been given the Rose Room, decorated in deep reds and greens and too much antique furniture, on which I bruise my knees as I unpack. My car-cramped body is aching from the long drive, so I stretch out on the saggy bed. Anxiety soon drives me out of the room and into the garden again, towards the piano. I thump out a Scott Joplin tune on the gap-toothed keyboard, trying to silence the voice in my head that keeps asking *what now?* Wallabies graze on the lush summer grass behind me, unmoved by my rusty ragtime.

Nella is our designated map-reader and that evening, while Andrew makes dinner for us, she plans our hiking schedule for the next five days. They've been in training for this trip, doing long walks every weekend. I've been swimming thirty laps a day for the past couple of months, but climbing mountains is very different from kicking gently through tepid water. Lack of sleep has left me permanently fatigued, and I'm worried about holding them back. It's been a long time since I tackled a twenty-five kilometre hike.

After dinner, back in my room, I climb into bed and study the maps, trying to imagine myself striding across the landscape like an alpine Amazon. When I'm ready to sleep I leave the bedside light on: this Amazon has become afraid of the dark. Or rather, of the terrors that invade her mind in the early hours.

In the morning I avoid the communal dining room. I eat a muesli bar in my room, then Andrew drives us back through Jindabyne and up to Charlotte's Pass. A noticeboard informs us that the pass is named after Charlotte Adams, the first woman of European descent to reach the summit of Mount Kosciuszko. Forget the Amazons—maybe I should be trying to channel Charlotte.

I pull out my phone and search: Charlotte made the climb in 1881, when she was twenty-one years old, accompanied by her father. Not long afterwards she married a man named Herbert. Other than the men in her life, my search tells me very little about Charlotte and nothing at all about the Indigenous Ngarigo women who might have climbed the peak before her. What were their names? What did they call this mountain? Wikipedia is silent.

I add an extra layer of clothing against the cool alpine wind and the three of us head for the Blue Lake. A path leads us down a steep hill towards a glinting river. In spite of the season there are still luminescent patches of snow on the distant peaks. Purple, white and yellow wildflowers are strewn beside the path as if from a giant's basket. We step across the river on wobbly rocks and as we begin the ascent towards Carruthers Peak my lungs start to burn. Good. When you're labouring for breath like this there's less energy for rumination. We stop to watch some children sliding down a patch of remnant snow, their faces flushed and animated, their pants soaking wet. I remember how this feels. When you're a child, the thrill of speed trumps any discomfort. I'm tempted to join them but there's still a long walk ahead of us.

An hour and a half later we descend along a narrow path to the Blue Lake which, with clouds piling up overhead, is actually slate grey. We huddle out of the wind, eating our sandwiches to the background roar of water rushing out of the lake towards the Snowy River. After lunch we follow the river until we reach a pool called Hedley Tarn, where Andrew suggests we cut across country to rejoin the track above the Blue Lake. I'm nervous. What if those grim clouds get lower? What if the fog comes down, or we're caught in a snow shower? Terrible things happen suddenly in the mountains. But Andrew is confident he knows where to go, and Nella is happy to join him. And I don't want to walk alone.

As we pick our way carefully across lichen-stained boulders I think about fearless Charlotte Adams, hiking these boggy meadows in her long wet skirts. Did she know she was making (settler) history up here? Was she looking forward to marrying Herbert? Did they go on to have children? They called pregnancy 'confinement' in those days. I wonder if motherhood curtailed her adventuring and confined her to home life. Did she miss stooping to inspect the infinite variety of cushiony grasses up here in the alps? Seeing herself reflected in the pools of melting snow?

The anxiety that has been clutching at me for weeks is also melting. By the time the three of us rejoin the main path and begin climbing out of the lake basin, I'm ready to try a spot of alpine yodelling, and launch into 'The Lonely Goatherd'. 'Yodel-odel-odel-odel-odel eh-hee-hoh,' I sing, opening my arms wide and spinning in slow Sufi circles. I am high, yes. On a hill—yes! It feels miraculous.

The next three days follow a similar pattern. Up early, pack our lunches, and drive to the starting point for a different day-walk. We hike to places with gothic names like Dead Horse Gap and Ram's Head Range. We find warm flat rocks and spread out our picnics, making up unlikely stories for each other about murdered ponies and severed sheep heads.

One day we follow a path along the Thredbo River, where flirting trout chase each other in circles just under the surface. We dare each other to wade into the icy water, hugging ourselves and laughing.

Another day we catch a chairlift to the top of Mount Kosciuszko and take in the 360-degree views of the Snowy Mountains banked up against the skyline. Then we walk down along a gently winding track through black and silver stands of snow gums. Fierce bushfires a few years ago have left these trees looking like bleached coral stranded thousands of metres above sea level. Will they come back to life?

One day we decide to give our weary bodies a rest. We sleep in, then drive to the edge of the Alpine National Park and find a quiet spot to lie on picnic blankets and read books all afternoon. In between chapters I watch a kingfisher defending its territory against wattlebird incursions. On the drive back, at dusk, we decide to pull over and walk down into a grassy valley, where a dozen wild brumbies stare at us in frozen panic before taking off into the forest.

I feel a surge of envy—if only I could take off when I wanted to, get away from my life, find a new place where I could be someone else. But why not? I am untethered. I have all this freedom now. Why not use it?

On the final day of our holiday the weather is steamy, a day for swimming. We drive into town and find a shady park beside Lake Jindabyne. The water is almost warm compared to the body-shock of Thredbo River. I wade in and strike out towards the middle of the lake, then stop and pedal my legs, looking back towards the sun-bleached fields surrounding the town of Jindabyne.

Treading water: that's how you deal with grief. Not waving, not drowning. Just staying afloat till you can catch your breath and you're ready to head back to shore.

submergence

EARLY IN 2012 I'm staying with my sister, still living
out of the suitcase I packed on the night the relationship
ended. Time to retrieve the rest of my stuff from my former
home. First I email Tom to make sure he won't be at home
that weekend, then I rent some storage space and book a
removal van.

The day I pack up my belongings there is a flood at his
house, a leak starting somewhere in the laundry. It takes me
a while to realise what's happening as I walk back and forth,
carrying heavy boxes, occasionally glancing at the water.
Eventually I stop and look more closely. It's a miniature
waterfall. The water is spreading all over the laundry floor
and will soon be out in the hallway.

About a year before this, I'd been thinking a lot about
floods. The nightly news at that time was full of natural

disasters: tsunamis, volcanic eruptions, islands drowning under rising sea levels. The climate change predictions were looking more and more dire, and the seaside suburb where we lived had been mentioned in dispatches. A century and a half ago it was a swamp, before European invaders turned it into a dump that stank of nightsoil and the waste from a nearby abattoir. Eventually canals were built to drain the oily water into the long-suffering bay. Now it's one of the most densely populated suburbs in Melbourne. And acutely vulnerable to the predicted high tides and floodwaters.

At the time the possibility of flooding preyed on my mind—what if all our food was washed away, and we couldn't buy more because all the shops had been flooded too?—so one day I packed a cane basket with tinned food, candles and matches, and took it upstairs to the girls' bedroom. There was a cavity in the ceiling up there which the girls had sometimes used as a cubby house when they were younger. The perfect place to store the basket. 'Apocalypse stocking', I called it.

Now, a year later, I can't work out how to fix this leak. I used to do all the repairs around here—the blown light globes, the loose screws, the jammed blinds. I stood on wobbly stools, knelt on creaking floorboards, patiently unpicked knots and glued things back together. But in this moment, as the water pools around my feet, I realise my fixing skills have limits. I begin throwing down towels—bath towels, tea towels, paper towels—anything that will soak up liquid. But it doesn't stop the flow and for a moment I am utterly at a loss.

I ring Tom's son, who tells me to turn the water off at the mains and call a plumber.

Of course. Just turn the water off.

Is this my fault? The pipe must have been leaking before I arrived, but somehow it feels like it will be blamed on me. I turn off the water and that's all I can do. This thing can't be fixed, not by me. The apocalypse has already arrived. Not, as I feared, in the form of a thundering flood but as a silent trickle, hidden from view. A trickling away to nothing.

Before leaving the house for the last time I climb the stairs to the girls' bedroom, stand on a wobbly stool, push open the hatch into the ceiling cavity and drag out the apocalypse stocking basket. It's coming with me.

severance

WHEN A LONG-TERM relationship ends in a large family, the ripples can be more like rogue waves. In the weeks and months following the break-up, emails pour into my inbox from members of Tom's clan—children, siblings, sisters-in-law, cousins, even ex-wives—all trying to work out what just happened. After ten years they'd finally relaxed their guard and assumed I was here to stay. Suddenly there's another woman overboard and everyone is flinging out lifebuoys.

Many of them go out of their way to make me feel as if I'm still part of the clan, inviting me for coffees, concerts, book-club gatherings, crying sessions. In the beginning I say yes to everything, clinging to whatever might keep me afloat. I love these people. They have become my family and my friends. But when they pass on news of a niece's promotion or a nephew's album launch, it's like receiving a telegram from a land whose borders are closed to me.

My greatest fear is losing Jay. I am no longer his de facto stepgrandmother. Who *am* I? His mother tells me that when they first visited Tom's house after I'd left, Jay asked 'Where's Sian?' over and over. 'Where has she gone?' *It's a mystery.*

Six months after the break-up I finally move out of Yoni's place. I've found a new home on the other side of town, not far from where Jay and his family live. Once a week I look after him for a few hours while his father is at work and his mother and baby brother sleep. We play ambulance games in the back of my hatchback, saving the lives of invisible patients with ockie straps and a car jack. He leads, I follow. Together we make a good team. Perhaps he will be a doctor.

When Jay turns four a big family celebration is planned. I'm invited but I can't face it, so Jay's mother organises a second 'party'. There are only two guests—me and one of Jay's great-aunts—and we have a small birthday cake, but it's awkward. Jay peers at us, trying to solve the mystery of our wet eyes. Still, I'm grateful. They're working so hard to keep me in the fold.

Sometimes I pick Jay up and drive him back to my place and play the clarinet for him. One day he announces he'd like to have a turn. Without thinking, I hand the instrument over. Stretching his mouth over the mouthpiece, Jay bites down, shattering the fragile bamboo reed with his sharp teeth. I realise in that moment how unused I am to the carelessness of children, their blissful ignorance of the damage they can do. Removing the broken reed I encourage him to sing into the mouthpiece instead, but he knows it's a sham. So I pull out a couple of recorders and we hoot out painful high notes together in my living room.

For lunch I boil him an egg, and he waves his yolk-dipped toast around, telling me all the things he's learning about the world. He loves nature documentaries and is apparently on first-name terms with David (Attenborough).

'Did you know, Sian,' he begins, then describes the latest astonishing ocean creature David has introduced him to. Sharks fascinate Jay, especially their sharp teeth, but he's also quite taken with the shape-shifting ways of the octopus. After lunch we look for turtles under the living-room couch, and we're both disappointed when it's time for me to take him home.

There comes a day when, invited to dinner by Jay's parents, I cycle up the hill to their place with a bottle of wine and discover they've forgotten about the invitation. I make light of it, cycle home again and drink the bottle of wine alone. Over the next few weeks, whenever I offer to babysit, there's always a great-aunt or a grandparent who's already volunteered ahead of me. My hurt is way out of proportion. Life with two small children is inevitably chaotic, and there are so many family members with a greater claim to Jay's time than me. But I'm hypersensitive to any possibility of rejection, so I back off. I wait for Jay's parents to contact me and, while waiting, I ruminate on what it was like to be part of the babysitting A-Team. Will it always be like this now? Me, off to the side, a distant satellite spinning around the centre of the family? I have no blood connection with Jay and, in this family, blood counts for a lot.

Tom's daughters are both young adults now. Not long after the break-up we'd met up to share sushi and tears, but finally the wicked stepmother reared her ugly head. My anger with their father spilled out, and now they're not responding to my text messages. We've known each other for more than a decade: I've watched them grow from small children into young women. But before I met them, they had already lived through their parents' divorce and maybe this latest breakage is one too many.

Tom's siblings have always shared enormous pride in his career successes, but now many of them are also deeply troubled by how he ended our relationship. Pride and shame can make for uncomfortable bedfellows: there comes a time when even those I'm closest to grow tired of feeling bad about what happened. More ruptures. I love these people, but right now it seems we can't be friends.

Is it injured pride that leads me to back away from Jay's little family? Or is it all just too painful? We stay in touch for a couple of years, but when I spend time with Jay and his brother and parents, I'm awash with paralysing contra-dictions—envy, gratitude, grief, anger, regret. And love.

My love for this child was hard-won. Now it's both unshakeable and intolerable. If I try to stay in Jay's life there will be constant reminders of all that I have lost. Eventually, in one of the hardest decisions I've ever made, I choose self-exile.

Seven years later I'm walking the dog on a weekday afternoon. The final bell rings out from the local primary school and soon there are clusters of kids mooching along the footpath, heading for home. A boy of about ten is walking towards us and I slow down, half-expecting him to stop and pat the dog, as most kids do, but he's looking at the ground and his pace doesn't slow. Just as he's passing us, he glances up from under a curtain of dark hair, straight into my eyes, and then he's behind us. I walk on for a few steps, then stop. That face. I swivel round, but the boy has turned the corner into a nearby alley and disappeared. I walk on, doing the maths. Jay was four when we last saw each other, which would make him eleven. My steps slow again.

Now I've turned again, tugging on the dog's lead, and we're hurrying back up the street and into the alley. No sign of the boy. I break into a half-jog, then back to a fast walk again. Don't want to scare him. At the end of the alley I can see him about fifty metres ahead of me. He looks back and now he's the one half-jogging, to get away from the crazy dog lady who's following him. He turns another corner and disappears, and I force myself to stop.

Was it him? A child's face can change dramatically in seven years. And if it was, what would I have said?

Hi, you might not remember me, but we used to go scuba diving in my living room, and you were sure there were a

few sea turtles under my couch, and I don't know if you're
still into David Attenborough documentaries, but I hope so.

Or would he be old enough to hear this version?

Hi, maybe you remember me, because we loved each other
and I tried so hard to stay in your life, but it turned out that
seeing you was harder than not seeing you, so I had to give
you up, and all I can say is sorry—sorry—sorry—sorry—

inexperience

WHEN MY FRIENDS were having kids, I longed for them to share their children with me. They knew about my 'situation'. I thought they would make the offers, issue the invitations. Perhaps they thought it would be too painful for me. And to be fair, I'm not the world's greatest sharer myself. For example, I have a spare room in my house, with a comfortable bed, a wardrobe, warm blankets. Most of the time the room remains empty, the door closed. I've thought about sharing my home, opening the door, welcoming someone in. But I haven't, or never for long. A few days here, a few months there, nothing permanent. I don't really want to share, not all the time. Was it the same with my friends and their children?

Of course, a child is not like a room. I didn't want to move in with my friends and their families. I just wanted to share in loving their kids, be invited to the birthday parties, the school concerts, the afternoons at the beach. I wanted to be the babysitter of choice, the pseudo-aunt. I offered, over and over. 'I'm here,' I told them. 'If you want some time off, I'd love to hang out with the kids.' They almost never asked.

One friend—like me—had struggled to have a child. She had described to me how gutted she was when her friends didn't invite her to their kids' special events. But when she finally did have a child, I was not invited to her daughter's birthday parties. I couldn't understand. But it feels shameful to crave such a thing, and I said nothing.

Sometimes I wondered if my friends didn't trust me to take good care of their children. The term 'helicopter parenting' was fashionable at the time, a pejorative description of the hypervigilance inspired by parental anxiety. Maybe the new parents of my generation found it hard to trust that their children would be safe unless they were in the care of someone they were related to. Or someone who already had a child of their own.

There were exceptions. Friends who invited me to stay at their beach house each summer, where their young daughters took turns sitting on my lap on the balcony, singing songs, laughing at my dumb jokes. Another friend who brought her little boys to my place, where I made them spiders and watched their jaws drop as the ice-cream frothed the lemonade into mini volcanoes. And my sister Yoni, who asked me to babysit her son, invited me to his school concerts and sent him off to the cinema with me on Saturday afternoons, where I bought him enormous buckets of popcorn. My nephew and I made up songs together, and played hide and seek in their backyard, and I always let him find me.

Years later, here's what I'm wondering—did I *really* make all those babysitting offers to my friends? Or did the shame—the fear of appearing needy—silence me? My desire for closeness with a child sometimes felt like quicksand. Perhaps my friends could hear the red-headed giant muttering whenever I was near (*fee fi fo fum!*) and thought he would come for their children.

That spare room of mine—I still don't understand why I've been so reluctant to share it. Have I been worried that the occupant would take up more space in my life than I wanted to offer them? Is this how my friends-who-were-parents felt about me?

difference

GRIEF CREATES a vacuum. It's not long before a man with brilliant green eyes comes along to fill the gap. He's smart, handsome and recently divorced. A father of three, a bushwalker, a musician and a lover of languages. His attention is a balm. We both have a new-found freedom. What shall we do with this strange gift?

In late September 2012 I travel to France for a work gig at a small arts festival. Afterwards the green-eyed man joins me and we go hiking together between medieval hilltop villages in the upside-down autumn. We amble past slow-munching cows and stone fences draped with blackberries. We snack on giant white meringues. We pass through almond orchards and stop to pick up fallen nuts. We visit a town that once housed a hospital for lepers, and I wonder whether they survived their banishment by forming a new tribe for themselves, a family of outcasts with missing bits. The next day the green-eyed man and I picnic beside the Dordogne, and I venture into the glinting water to test the strength of the current. No stronger than me, I tell myself, swimming hard against its rushing force.

As we're walking, we talk about his God and my godlessness. I begin to understand that, despite everything we have in common, nothing is as important to him as this thing we don't share. He tells me stories about his family, about how much his European mother suffered in her childhood, and how her suffering trickled down to the next generation. How he's trying to understand her better because that's what his God has advised.

Eating has been tricky for me in the past year, but the hotels we stay in serve us three-course meals dripping with butter, and I shovel food into my mouth like a starving woman. Sleeping has been hard too, and after hiking more than twenty kilometres each day, my body is as weary as it has ever been. Surely now I will be able to sleep? But at night my mind still struggles to rest. Sometimes I wake in the early hours and weep, counting off the things I have lost. The man with green eyes doesn't turn away.

One day we visit a chasm, a gaping hole in the earth that leads down to a vast complex of limestone caves. We're swallowed by the yawning entrance—Jonah into the whale—our eyes gradually adjusting to the darkness. There's a subterranean river down here, and we travel by boat past backlit stalactites that look like dripping sorbets. I want to dive into the cold black water and swim towards the centre of the earth, but the boatman warns us that people have got themselves lost in these wet crevices and never found a way out. I remind myself there's a sunny day awaiting us above this dark world, and there will be no women overboard here.

The final day of our walking tour takes us along a canyon, at the end of which a town appears to be clinging to a rockface. Is it a magic trick? A mirage? The closer we get, the better I understand how this gravity-defying architecture can be possible. Picks, bricks and mortar—and a firm belief in the existence of heaven—that's all you need to conquer nature.

Climbing the steep main street, we pass seven sanctuaries carved into sheer rock, and I think about the pilgrims and penitents who've been climbing this hill for ten centuries. Possibly I too am a pilgrim here, searching for something new to believe in now that my tribe has gone; but more likely a penitent, trying to forgive myself for the sin of self-delusion. It's hard not to feel like I've squandered the last ten years of my life. What a waste of precious time.

We climb 223 stone steps up the hill—the green-eyed man counts them—and arrive at a church dedicated to a woman they call the mother of God. How would that have been, to give birth—literally—to a belief system that would last for centuries? No medical interventions necessary there—not even a sperm donor, apparently.

The man with green eyes doesn't appreciate my jokes about the Virgin. There is silence between us as we descend the hill. Again I feel the gulf widening between the believer and the unbeliever, and wonder if it can be bridged.

It takes another six months, but eventually I have to concede the answer is no. The children of the green-eyed man are believers too, and they fear I will lead him away from the path of righteousness. Family dinners are awkward. When one of the children says grace, I feel like a fake. Worse, the green-eyed man's God disapproves of my gay friends.

There is a schism. There are injuries of the heart—of two hearts. I am sad, he is angry. We cannot be friends.

malevolence

IT'S LATE 2012 and I'm back on the radio, doing arts reviews. I spend my nights in theatres and cinemas, absorbing the stories of other people's lives as a way of escaping my own. Each fortnight I head into the radio station to talk about what I've seen. But even when I'm working there's no escaping the ghosts of lost children.

Many of the Australian films I'm invited to review this year tell gruelling tales of young people suffering. There are the hungry petrol-sniffing teenagers in *Samson and Delilah,* hiding under a bridge in the dry Todd River. There's a lost sister and a bullying father in *Beautiful Kate.* In *Blessed* there are vulnerable children wandering the streets, stealing from shopping malls and posing naked for the prurient camera. In the claymation film *Mary and Max,* the loneliness of the girl Mary reduces me to tears.

It's the same on the stage. I watch a theatre production in which a young boy witnesses an act of violence towards his mother, then rehearses the trauma over and over with toys. Another play, set in the year 2039, has characters who are grappling with the intergenerational fallout of child abuse in the midst of a climate apocalypse. Then there's a puppet show in which three small children are hunkered down in front of a television watching wildlife documentaries while their drunken mother entertains her violent boyfriend. Fantasy is their only refuge, and they dream about transforming themselves into dangerous animals like lions and leopards.

I think about Jay and our turtle-spotting games in my loungeroom. Maybe your imagination can only be filled with gentle creatures if you live in a gentle family. This puppet show, the program tells me, is based on a true story. Watching the final scene, I'm weeping again as a puppet child crouches alone on the stage, abandoned. How could someone who is lucky enough to have a child betray that child so terribly? And why are all these stories being told *now*? Are they sounding a warning, exposing something that is all around us, but which we refuse to see?

When I pose these questions to the afternoon radio host, he winces. This isn't the cheerful cultural commentary he was hoping for. Terrible tales about terrorised tots will not help his ratings, and he winds up the segment before I can tell him about the research I've been doing. Turns out these performances are mirroring what's happening in real life. Here in Australia, real children are increasingly depressed, anxious, drunk, neglected, abused, violent and suicidal. I've found statistics showing that the number of children reported to child protection departments for abuse and neglect has doubled in the last decade. Suicide rates for adolescent boys have increased four-fold since the 1960s, and the rates for adolescent girls have doubled in that time. Psychological problems in young people, binge drinking, attempted suicide and aggressive crimes are all on the rise, and the figures for young Indigenous people are even higher. A recent state ombudsman's report painted a horrifying picture of the child protection system, illustrating the rising statistics for child homicides with nightmarish case studies. I feel like I've stumbled into a Hieronymus Bosch painting.

Parents are not solely to blame for the terrible things happening to their children. There are so many obstacles to care and kindness. More and more people in this lucky country are living in poverty. More and more parents are struggling with overwork, unemployment, insecure jobs, debt, racism, cultural dislocation, technological bafflement, chronic illness, substance abuse, their own childhood traumas—the list is endless. Parenting is hard in a hardening society.

But that shameful part of my brain—childlike, resentful—can't let go of the idea that something terribly unfair has happened if people who are unfit or unable to care for their children are producing them with ease while I remain childless. I wouldn't have let my child suffer in the way the children behind these terrible statistics are suffering. At least, this is what I am trying to believe.

recurrence

IT'S 2013 and once again I'm lying semi-naked on a medical examination table with a gynaecologist between my legs. He's trying to find out what's been causing me to bleed so copiously in recent months. I'm forty-nine and the obvious suspect is perimenopause, but as my GP says, 'It's always best to check.' So here's another medico probing my insides for the solution to a mystery.

After a while he looks at me from between my knees, grinning, and says, 'Well that's good news! You have plenty of healthy-looking eggs in there!'

I stare at him. On what planet is it *good news* for a childless, previously infertile perimenopausal woman approaching fifty to be told she now has *plenty of eggs*?

—

Meanwhile, I've met a man I like, a curly-haired musician. Every time he sits down at the piano he seems to reinvent what music can be. He owns a huge black dog and when he goes out at night, it scratches deep gashes in his back door, trying to escape. The dog has also destroyed the seatbelts in his ute. I worry about bodies flying through windscreens, but the curly-haired man is in no rush to get the seatbelts fixed. His family unit has recently disintegrated, and when he talks about missing his daughters he becomes short of breath.

He tells me he craves an improvisational life. He'd like to be able to reinvent himself every day of the week, with no repeats. Right now, without a job, he has the freedom to do just that. I look in my diary at the lists of work commitments, rehearsals, board meetings—the responsibilities I seem to collect like his dog collects burrs. Perhaps I am less free than I thought.

The curly-haired man used to believe in the same God as the green-eyed man, and his parents still do. When he was a child his mother believed his powers of invention were the Devil's work. He laughs as he's telling me about it, but I can hear that it's not funny to him. Sometimes his grief seems to go even deeper than mine.

It's not going to work. The curly-haired man is too improvisational for someone like me. And perhaps we are both too sad for each other.

—

In the wake of this latest rupture, I find myself wondering about the mothers of these men I keep falling for. About how hard it must be to know whether you are doing motherhood 'right'. And I wonder if I'd have been the kind of mother I expected. I might have been less loving. Or determined to change the essence of my child, or unable to overcome my own fear and sadness, and therefore fated to pass it on. I wonder how much of the fear and sadness in me can be traced back to the rogue wave that took my father away, leaving my brilliant mother alone and afraid.

Margot has recently begun writing about her life. She's in her seventies now and is worrying about her memory. She wants to get her stories down in case they disappear. Sometimes she shyly shows me her notes. In one draft chapter she has written about how much my brother David looks like our father Glen, and how painful it has been, at times, seeing her dead husband in her son's young face.

'Children,' she writes, 'are at once the most glorious and the most searing experience one ever has. This is the only life after death that I can comprehend—transmission of oneself to one's children. The childless have no life after death once memory fades.'

That last sentences rankles. *Isn't it why you're writing your memoirs, so your stories will live on after your death?* These pages are not just an insurance policy against a fading memory. They are a legacy.

But I'm worried she might perceive my questions as

criticisms, so I say nothing. Knowing what she must have endured after our father disappeared, I've never felt comfortable criticising her. Like every other mother I've observed, Margot has sometimes wondered out loud about whether she has 'failed' in some way at motherhood. Perhaps this is an inevitable part of being a parent—imperfection anxiety in the face of impossible standards.

Through all those years I spent trying to have a child, I thought giving birth would stop me feeling like a failure. Probably it would just have been the beginning of a different way of failing.

~

When I was young my grandmother Peg used to sing me songs about the sea. One went like this:

> We joined the navy to see the sea
> And what did we see?
> We saw the sea.
> We saw the Pacific and the Atlantic
> And the Atlantic wasn't romantic
> And the Pacific wasn't what it's cracked up to be.

I loved those rhyming lines, those alliterative s-es, but it always struck me as odd that Peg sang me this song about oceanic disappointment. She couldn't get enough of the sea. Her favourite place was on a surf beach, striding along at low tide in her floral bathing suit and her terry-towelling beach coat, a dog at her heels, a grandchild rushing ahead to find the best rockpools.

Perhaps the song was meant as a warning, like those fairytales where the happy ending never comes. *Beware of your fantasies, my girl. They will get you in trouble.*

effluence

IN 2013 my body decides it's had enough of pointless fertility and it's time for menopause. Such a strange word, the way it contains both *men* and *pause.* Is it a sign? *Should* I give men a pause? Even stranger is the fact that menopause doesn't signal a *pause* at all: it's *The End*—a full stop.

The dreaded hot flushes are not too bad, but the waves of rage are disconcerting and the unpredictable bleeding is a nightmare. My GP prescribes the contraceptive pill to regulate my body's sudden flooding. 'Take it for a year,' the doctor says, 'and when you come off it, I predict menopause will be over.'

I'm not ready to give men a pause. I meet a square-jawed man who loves words as much as I do. He writes for hours, hunched at his desk, churning out screenplays and short stories and sending me emails that make me laugh for days.

He has an adult son and an ex-wife who live in another state, and right now he has so much freedom he's not sure what to do with it. While I hurtle towards my deadlines, he's in no hurry to finish things. 'You're good at *doing*,' he tells me, 'but I'm good at *being*.'

Is he right? Could I find a way to do more *being,* or is that an oxymoron? Perhaps I could step away from those deadlines and spend more time studying seashells by the seashore.

Six months after the square-jawed man and I get together, I go off the pill. A few months later there's still been no bleeding. 'There are two possibilities,' I tell him. 'Either it's all over, red rover, or I'm pregnant.'

It's a lame joke. He knows my history. Still, he gives me a strangely familiar look: of tenderness, perhaps even hope. *Would* he be willing to have a child with me, if I *was* pregnant?

His only son had nearly died in infancy, the boy's tiny brain invaded by a rare cancer. After the baby endured gruelling and apparently unsuccessful treatment in a city hospital, the square-jawed man and his wife took their boy home to die. He shakes his head as he's relating this story, as if trying to dislodge the images from his memory. I can't begin to imagine the terror he must have felt, the strength it would have taken just to get up every morning. But the treatment *did* work and the child survived. Every time their son celebrates a birthday, he tells me, it feels like a miracle.

It would be another miracle if I *was* finally pregnant at the age of forty-nine.

Reader, I was not.

—

It's 2019 and I'm having lunch with a friend who does woodworking as a hobby. She's showing me some photos of tiny wooden boxes lined in velvet, some blue, some pink. She's making coffins, she explains, for babies that have miscarried or were stillborn. She calls them Angel Boxes—gleaming rectangular caskets of cypress, walnut and camphor laurel, each about the size of a jewellery box. 'Some parents use them for burying their babies,' she says, 'and some use them to store keepsakes associated with the child.'

I stare at the photos, trying to picture what I might have kept inside one of those boxes. Would my three early miscarriages have been worthy of such beautiful vessels? We never chose names for them. After the first miscarriage, I tried not to allow myself that degree of attachment. Names were among many things I didn't allow myself to plan for, just in case. They were potentialities. Fantasies. Hopes.

independence

IN 2014 I sell my old car and buy a small delivery van. My stepfather John has offered to convert it into a mini camper-van for me. He's made and sold at least five campervans over the decades, and my parents have crisscrossed the continent many times in their houses-on-wheels. My van is not just a new toy. It's the outcome of a conversation I've been having with myself, about loss, safety and solitude.

Having a child would have given me lifelong connection and communion—this is what I believed. Someone in whose mind I would be ever-present. Someone who would be ever-present in my mind. A tethering, a tugging back to the world. Without that child I feel untethered, a balloon let go by a careless hand. Sometimes this feeling is assuaged by a singing rehearsal, a meal with a friend, a night with a lover. Sometimes I can tether myself to nature, sitting quietly beside a creek or bobbing with seagulls in the ocean. But a wintry wind is always coming, ready to blow me back into that cold, high place.

I'm trying to persuade myself that this is not a childlessness thing—it's a human thing. I'm not alone in feeling alone. But how can I find a way to feel safe with my solitude? How can I convert my freedom into something positive? What choices do I have *because* of not getting what I most wanted? Right now, all my work—teaching, writing, mentoring, singing—is freelance and flexible. Much of it is also portable. I have no dependents, and my home can be rented out to cover the mortgage. Most of my friends are busy raising teenagers. Perhaps this freedom is the consolation prize for all that I've lost. The campervan will allow me to be near the sea whenever I want, with countless fathoms of ocean to swim in.

My stepfather's plan for the van is a marvel of economic design, dreamt up in the wakeful hours octogenarians endure after midnight. We construct it together in his back shed—the master and his apprentice. He builds a bed base and some wooden benches at the back, under which we slide a couple of recycled drawers. I buy a foam mattress and some cushions, and John creates ingenious storage compartments under the bed, including a long drawer he handcrafts from found timber. It's perfect for storing bird books and binoculars, sunscreen and sandals. I sew together flyscreens for the windows with old op-shop table runners. The cutlery comes from a picnic basket I scored at a swap night. We add a single-burner stove to the 'kitchen', a plastic water container and a fire extinguisher. When John quizzes me about whether I know how to use the fire extinguisher, I fudge, telling him the square-jawed man definitely knows how to use one, so we'll be fine. John stares at me, deadpan. 'What if *he's* on fire?'

I learn how to use the fire extinguisher.

My mother hears an interview on the radio with a writer called Beth Spencer, who's written a collection of poems about her year in a campervan. Margot buys me a copy of *Vagabondage*, and I immerse myself in these poetic reflections on the travelling life. In one poem called 'Loving stuff' the author writes:

> *Have I become one of those*
> *people who*
> *used to have people*
> *but now have stuff?*
> *Things*
> *are safer*
> *(people,*
> *so complicated)…*
> *And they don't*
> *suddenly announce one day*
> *they are leaving.*

Have *I* become one of those people? My house is full of stuff—books, musical instruments, cushions, wine glasses, pot plants, framed photos, nail files. So many things share my space, but I still live alone. The square-jawed man is renting a room in a nearby suburb, and sometimes he wonders aloud about us living together. I'm not ready. What if he's one of those people who suddenly announce one day they are leaving—or just…leave, like my drowned father?

Over the summer holidays we do some van trips together, driving south down the freeway and camping by the coast. There are dawns and sunsets accompanied by the rhythmic crashing of waves. There's the hazy horizon stretching further than my ageing eyes can see clearly. And there's the pleasure of being physically contained within a tiny space. The van is the length of a station wagon, the living area the size of a double bed. In there I feel safe, cocooned, confined. The square-jawed man and I lie back on the cushions, reading novels and sipping coffees brewed on the little stove. I take photos of the sea with my phone and send them to envious friends back in town.

Small pleasures feel like grand discoveries. Finding a shady tree on a warm afternoon. Staying in a camp-park dotted with eucalypts, which are dotted with dozing koalas. Walking along a jetty where pelicans perch like avian sentinels atop whitewashed poles. Discovering a tiny beach around a rocky corner with just one set of footprints leading across the dry sand—but whose? At night the square-jawed man and I fall asleep salty from the surf and wake up with stiff, mad hair. I'm a child in a cubbyhouse again, hiding from adult demands. It's like leaving home but taking my home with me—minus all the Stuff.

We visit the coastal village where I spent so many childhood holidays staying in my grandmother's beach shack. The beach is smaller now, and not just because I am bigger. The encroaching tides have washed away most of the dunes where my cousins and I used to play, scalding our feet in the hot sand. The surf life-saving club has been demolished and rebuilt—the ocean was lapping at its foundations. Now, instead of a small fibro building, there's a grand new brick edifice, further from the shoreline and fortified against the rising seas. Walking the beach, I remember the mysteries that preoccupied me four decades ago. Were catfish cats or fish? Why did the tides come in and out, but never at exactly the same time each day? Did the seagulls leave feathers on the beach especially so I could collect them for my mum? I remember the young girl who befriended me one day as we played in the shallow pools left by the tide, and how I rushed back to tell Mum about her. 'Her name is Certificate!' My mother smiled. 'Are you sure?' I ran back to my friend to check, then returned with a small correction. 'It's Felicity.' Those syllables just needed to be put in the right order.

Back in town, as summer bleeds into autumn, the square-jawed man and I begin planning a trip up north in the van. We'll escape the cold Melbourne winter, embrace our freelancing freedom. But I'm starting to wonder about this man. There's something unreachable about him, and my occasional surges of menopausal rage don't help.

Perhaps he finds it hard to feel safe with me. When he was growing up his mother was often ill and absent. His father, a war veteran, did his best to care for their six children, but he had his own demons. The square-jawed man and I both had a parent who was there one minute, gone the next. We're an uneasy combination. A childless mother can be a smothering lover, and a man who missed his mother can be an anxious lover.

There is another rupture. We're both angry, both sad. Perhaps we will be friends, later. I hope so. But I'm not sure how many more breakages I can bear.

I've rarely felt safe with solitude. Loneliness has been the shark beneath the waves, stalking me through the decades. Love has hauled me out of harm's way over and over again, but it's not working anymore. I'm fifty years old now, well into the age when people bandy the words mid-life crisis around. I've never liked the term, the way it reduces a difficult conversation with yourself to a histrionic headline. It's not a crisis, it's a time of reckoning, and mine has arrived.

concordance

IT'S 2015, I'm driving north in the van and Paul Simon is singing sweetly on my CD player about the ways to leave your lover and I'm thinking there are more than fifty and none of them are sweet. My house has been rented out for three months to a young couple who are expecting a baby. I'm trying not to feel like the universe is playing a trick on me. My home will be the very first home of *someone else's* very first child. Will the place be warm enough for a newborn in winter? I pull over and text the tenants to remind them about the spare heater in the wardrobe.

I won't be needing heaters for a while. My destination is Queensland, the state of my birth and the place I've always blamed for my loathing of cold weather. Born in Brisbane in late August, I was bathed for the first year of my life in humid warmth. But in the wake of my father's death, the remnants of our family fled south to chilly Melbourne. Since I've been an adult, misery has descended on me every winter while I count the days until spring. Now that I have the van, I can pretend winter doesn't exist.

In a small town in north-west New South Wales, I stop for a stroll down the main street. A sandstone clock tower throws a long shadow from the middle of a roundabout, one side of it inscribed with the names of dead soldiers. I pause to read a street sign covered in hieroglyphics, strange wedge-shaped strokes like an ancient Sumerian script. *Stock Brands of the Liverpool Plains*, the title tells me. Next to the hieroglyphics is a list of names—*Known Early Squatters*—and all but one is a man. As I wander along the deserted street, I notice all the names on all the buildings—lawyers' offices, hotel proprietors, automotive repairs—are men's names. The population of this town, another sign tells me, is 2580, but most of the shopfronts are empty, their metal awnings rusting.

I'm here to give a book talk at the birthday party of one of the oldest regional book clubs in Australia. Like me, the club has turned fifty. The members have published a booklet about their history that tells me five decades ago an American woman blew into town, university-educated and newly married to a local grazier. She was a big reader and quickly found some bookish female friends in the local community. Many of these women lived outside the town, on farms where the soil was good and the crops bountiful, but female company was scarce and they struggled with loneliness. The American woman had apparently planned to be a diplomat, until love intervened. She knew how to run a meeting. And so, in 1965, the Book Club was formed.

There was a strict but sensible list of rules. Membership would be limited to thirty women. Everyone would take a turn at hosting a meeting and reviewing the books. One inaugural member describes herself in the booklet as having been a farmer's wife, living in 'an isolated new corner on a property (with) no hours to spare'. Then came a phone call from the brisk American: 'You will always find time, if you really want to do something.' It was a chance for the farmer's wife to pursue her great love of reading, to share books and ideas—and a space for women to gather where no one would interrupt them while they were speaking. The spare hours were duly found.

At the first meeting five decades ago, the booklet tells me, Patrick White and George Johnston were up for discussion. Over the ensuing years the quieter members were given gentle encouragement to overcome their fear of public speaking. When their turn came around, they discovered they could give impassioned presentations about literature. After about five hundred meetings, the club members have now discussed over seven hundred books. The oldest living member—one of the originals—is in her nineties.

The fiftieth anniversary is being celebrated at the local golf club. The walls of the dining room are decorated with plaques inscribed with the names of men who've won prizes for hitting a small ball with a long stick. Some of the book club members have invited their husbands to the party, and most of the men stand in clusters, talking about their parched soil. One of the husbands approaches me, wanting to find out what I know about the Australian poet Dorothea Mackellar. Her family owned a farm not far from here, he tells me, and the famous line 'I love a sunburnt country, a land of sweeping plains' was inspired by this area. The next line, the one about droughts, is a bit too close for comfort right now, he says. They're enduring one of the worst droughts the region has ever experienced. The watered greens outside the clubhouse windows are a lush emerald, but just beyond the arc of the sprinklers the ground is a dull brown as far as the eye can see.

I've been reading about this drought in the newspapers, and about the local member of parliament who denies any link with climate change, instead recommending prayer as the solution to these farmers' problems. The climate scientists see it differently, pointing to even worse droughts going on in California and Ethiopia right now, and reminding us that their modelling has been predicting that climate change would cause more droughts like these. When I mention this to the farmer who loves his sunburnt country, his face closes up and he moves away.

Today the men are outnumbered by silver-haired women. One by one they come up to me, clasp my hand and tell me how much the book club has meant to them. They use words like *stimulation, company, nourishment, insight.* I've recently published a book about social anxiety, and they've asked me to talk about how these fears can reduce people to silence, and how socially anxious people can be helped. I think they know the answers already.

'In your book club,' I tell them at the end of my speech, 'you've assuaged each other's loneliness, stimulated each other's minds, eased each other's fears. You've found your voices and allowed others to find theirs. You've created a wonderful legacy.'

As I drive away from the golf club that afternoon, I'm thinking about the word *legacy*, and whether I will leave one. Not in the form of children, obviously. Most of my professional output—newspaper articles, radio interviews, university lectures, singing recitals—has been ephemeral. My book about social anxiety will no doubt be superseded by another one on the same subject. Will anything I've done last beyond my lifetime? A choir I started twenty-five years ago is still going strong, and the book club I formed ten years ago still meets once a month. But there are no guarantees that these creations will endure. *Legacy. Progeny. Dynasty.* We accord these words so much weight and dignity, and when I consider them I feel as weightless as sea spume.

My mother the professor has created two kinds of legacies—her three children, and her research in child psychology, work that has helped countless other people's children lead better lives. The public record of her professional legacy will endure well after she's gone. She will be remembered. Is this what I crave? To be alive in someone's memory when I'm dead? To be commemorated on a plaque somewhere? I have no belief in an afterlife. Death will be an unending dreamless sleep. What difference will it make to the world if I die leaving nothing behind—or if I had never been born?

These thoughts can sometimes take me to a very dark place, but right now they're painless, abstract. Perhaps constant movement is the best defence against existential anxiety. Nothing matters too much when you keep leaving everything behind.

resistance

HEADING UP THE EAST coast, I stop at the Dorrigo National Park, a rainforest just out of Coffs Harbour in northern New South Wales, and a familiar name from my long-ago career as a greenie. Environmentalists campaigned for decades to protect this forest from logging, and now it's a World Heritage–listed national park, part of the largest strip of diverse rainforest in the world. I consult a map at the information centre and head off along the Blackbutt Track, lined with sculptured aerial tree roots and pretty epiphytes that cling to their host trees like infants to their mothers. It's a living museum of natural history, this forest. Ancient species of primitive conifers have survived here for thousands of years, their evolution halted by isolation. Scientists keep discovering small mammals they thought were extinct: Lazarus creatures—dead one minute, alive the next. As I walk under the shade of the mottled coachwood trees, I keep an eye out for these shy mammals, camera at the ready. Every now and then a brush turkey crosses the path ahead of me, a miniature dinosaur, kicking through leaves, but the mammals remain hidden, waiting for the humans to disappear. I don't blame them.

Later, studying a leaflet from the information centre, I find out that these rainforests had only just received their World Heritage status when I began working for the Australian Conservation Foundation in 1987. Back then, while many of my workmates were lobbying for national parks, I was more focused on the trashing of the ozone layer. In 1990 I joined an ACF delegation of ten young Australians to attend a United Nations conference in London. Humans had been pumping out ozone-depleting chemicals for decades and we wanted them to call a halt, before the ozone layer disappeared. The youngest member of our delegation was a seventeen-year-old schoolgirl called Zanny. One night during the conference, the ten of us got together in the lobby of our cheap hotel and wrote a speech, pleading with the UN delegates to take urgent action. The next morning, young Zanny stood behind a fancy wooden lectern and delivered our speech to government representatives from all over the globe. Then we took turns doing interviews with international journalists, pointing out that it was *our* generation who would suffer the most if governments failed to act.

Not long after, in a rare example of global coopera-tion, the signatories to that UN protocol agreed to phase out ozone-depleting chemicals. I don't imagine our small contribution had much to do with a major development in international diplomacy, of course, but still: it remains something to be proud of. Is this another way to think about legacy? Perhaps this kind of labour—advocating for the protection of nature—is the most important human legacy of all.

Our group stayed in touch for a while, and many of those young people remained politically active. The Canberra delegate went on to work as an advisor for a green-leaning political party. The Sydney delegate became the head of a successful Californian solar electricity company. One of the Melbourne delegates became a scientist, publishing research on the lizards and snails who live in rainforests like Dorrigo. And young Zanny became an artist, making work about urban sustainability and the environmental costs of globalisation. Last time I heard from her, she was working with kids in a high-security juvenile detention centre, finding ways for them to express their fear and loneliness inside that institutional black hole. Some of them were as young as ten years old. There are hundreds of these kids around the country, locked up in detention every night, and most of them are Indigenous. Angry, bored, frustrated, vulnerable kids, whom the prison system calls clients and the tabloid columnists call monsters.

The jailed kids are not the only ones the columnists are afraid of. I've been following the progress of Greta Thunberg, the Swedish teenager who started the global School Strike for Climate movement. Millions of other teenagers around the world have since joined her, protesting against political inaction on climate change. Greta has been vilified by conservative media commentators. One of them wrote: 'I have never seen a girl so young and with so many mental disorders treated by so many adults as a guru.' Another has called her a 'teenage puppet' and a 'climate bedwetter'. She looks like a 'cult member', wrote yet another. She's an 'annoying brat', 'hysterical', 'mentally unstable' and 'chilling'. Such visceral contempt feels a lot like a cover for shame.

Sometimes I hear people speaking about their own child with something like contempt in their voices. Their kid is *lazy* or *selfish* or *lacks initiative*. Their kid sleeps in too late, or won't look for a job, or seems to speak a language the parent doesn't understand. Sometimes, at the heart of that contempt, I sense disappointment that their child is not more like them. Or perhaps they're too much like them for comfort. Or perhaps they are afraid for their child's future.

I bite down on the impulse to tell them how lucky they are even to have a child.

⁓

I'm lying in the back of the van one night, scrolling through social media posts, when a video pops up of a child sobbing inconsolably. I can't look away. Bad people, he's discovered, are cutting down trees and killing animals. He's going to fight them, he yells at the camera, when he grows up! His grief is so fierce, so raw, I feel like a voyeur. Who is filming this? A parent? *Put the camera down,* I want to say. *Give that child a hug.* But the camera is steady, the vision unrelenting.

percipience

I'VE MADE IT TO Byron Bay. On the drive up the sea played peekaboo with me as the road curled past one glorious beach after another. In contrast, I'm jarred by the stories I've been hearing on the van radio. Two years ago—not long after I'd seen all those plays and films about terrified kids—the Australian Federal Government set up a Royal Commission into Institutional Responses to Child Sexual Abuse. Over the past twelve months the commission's public hearings have excavated thousands of horrific personal stories. Most of the assaults took place within religious institutions, at the hands of the adults the children had been schooled to respect.

Now the media is transfixed, and journalists are covering these stories in gruesome detail day after day. One Catholic schoolteacher in a Queensland country town sexually assaulted at least forty-four children. Many of the victims have been left with mental scars that will never heal. Some have attempted suicide, and quite a few have succeeded. Listening to the broken voices of their parents on the radio, I feel almost grateful for my childlessness. How could you survive a thing like that?

There are scars outside the van window, too—injuries to the landscape caused by roadworks on the Pacific Highway. Great gashes stripe the hillsides. Giant front-end loaders shunt piles of felled trees aside like a croupier pushing chips across the baize. Every time I pass one of these huge machines, I think about how much Jay loved 'diggers', and about the fact that he would now be the same age as some of the abused children they're discussing on the radio.

The Byron Bay house I'm staying in belongs to my friend Cameron. We first met when I was working for the ACF, and Cameron is still campaigning for the environment. He spends most of his time overseas, working for Greenpeace. Right now he's in New Zealand and he's offered me his home for a few weeks. The property backs onto the Arakwal National Park, so I wake each morning to birdsong. And rain. It's been raining off and on here for days. Such generous deluges. Hills become waterfalls, roads become rivers. potholes lie in wait on every street, perilous for a little van with fairly ordinary suspension.

Cameron has told me about the political battles going on in this beachside town over how to respond to the threats posed by rising sea levels. The developers and beachfront homeowners want to put up barricades against the erosion that will eventually ruin the town's tourist economy. Others argue that no barricades can hold back the rising sea. The main beach here definitely looks smaller than when I last visited. 'It's only a matter of time before that beach is gone,' Cameron told me. 'Much of this area is reclaimed swampland, and parts of the town are at sea level, so if a king tide breaches the dunes, the main street could go under.'

When it finally stops raining, I walk into the town centre to do some shopping and try to imagine what this street would look like under water. The top floors of the elegant old pubs in the main street would remain dry but, as in Venice, the owners might have to give up on the ground floors.

At the supermarket I search out my usual deodorant (baby-powder scented) and some sunscreen (for kids) and a pink moisturiser (especially for baby), products that make me feel safer. Part of my brain assumes there can be nothing harmful in them—no nasty chemicals, for example—because what kind of manufacturer would sell people something harmful meant for their babies? It's nuts, of course. If we can't keep children safe in Christian religious institutions, what makes me think we can keep them safe from capitalist corporations? I peer at the label on the back of the moisturiser. There are nineteen different chemicals listed in tiny print and, in larger print, the words *care*, *precious*, *indulgent* and *radiant*. I put the bottle back on the shelf.

In the afternoon I walk to the main beach, planning to swim. The water is still murky from the downpours, so instead I do a long walk. Watching parents and toddlers playing in the wet sand, I think about the word *baby*, and how often it's detached from its literal meaning. All those songs where lovers call each other 'baby'. Has it become a term of endearment because where there are babies there is always love? Or because with babies there are no barriers—and that's what we long for in love? Or is it a promise to take care of someone as you would care for an infant?

For decades I've carried a folded-up piece of paper in my wallet on which, at the age of twenty, I copied down a quote on the subject of love that seemed important to me at the time. About once a decade I pull out these words, from the Canadian-American feminist Shulamith Firestone, and read them again: roll them around in my brain to see what can be gleaned.

> Contrary to popular opinion, love is not altruistic.
> Love is the height of selfishness: the Self attempts
> to enrich itself through the absorption of another
> being...enjoying himself through the other instead
> of being one, locked in the cell of himself with only
> his experience and view, he could participate in the
> existence of another—an extra window on the world.

I don't know why I was so struck by these ideas all those years ago. Perhaps they contained a nugget of wisdom I thought I might understand better in the future. Perhaps a baby was meant to be my escape from 'the cell of myself'.

The word *baby* pops up in so many metaphors. *Take baby steps*, we say when something seems too hard. Acknowledge your fear and vulnerability but press on in spite of them. *Don't be a crybaby. He's such a man-baby. Stop babying her.* Most of these are about vulnerability too, even when they're used as insults.

I still have a couple of baby teeth. My dentist taps them fondly every time he sees me and whispers, 'Still going strong.' There are gaps around them, spaces that should have been filled by bigger teeth. I once did an internet search for 'adults with baby teeth'. *Tooth agenesis*, it's called. The adult teeth that should have come in are missing, so nothing forces the baby ones out of the way. 'A baby tooth that never fell out can sit happily in the mouth for decades,' the website told me.

Does it *mean* anything, the fact that I still have some baby teeth, and have never grown wisdom teeth? Maybe that's why I need this folded-up piece of paper: someone else's words of wisdom lodged in my wallet, ready to fill the gaps.

defence

I'VE DRIVEN TO a regional town in New South Wales where a friend of mine is staying with her sister. When I arrive at the family's lakeside property, the two women come rushing out of the house together and peer inside the little van, ooh-ing and aah-ing with approval. 'I need to get myself a caravan!' my friend announces. Like me, she's in her fifties. Like me, she's had miscarriages and no children. Like me, she has bucketloads of freedom. She's been using her freedom to travel the world and now has friends on every continent.

That evening, as we're eating dinner, the sister's husband grumbles about how their daughter—who's about to have her first baby—is planning to go back to work 'too soon', in his opinion.

'Maybe she's worried about losing her job,' I suggest, 'and

her income, and her career.' I'm surprised by my vehemence. Working women with children are not my 'tribe'. When politicians and media commentators use phrases like 'working mums', 'working families' and 'mum-and-dad investors' I feel obliterated. Why am I arguing with this stranger, sticking up for a young woman I've never met? Maybe I see my ghost self in her situation: the one who got the child she wanted—and then had to choose between the lesser of several evils.

'I'm happy to pay more taxes so women can stay home with their babies as long as they want to,' I tell him, '*and* so they can go back to work whenever they want to, with free childcare. Working women are told they can have it all, but it's just not true.' My tone almost spoils the evening, but the sister quickly moves the conversation on to their financial investments.

The next day, while my friend and her sister go shopping for gifts for the imminent grandchild, I take a walk around the local lake. It's a windless sunny day, and there are ducks mirrored in the still water. I pass half-a-dozen pairs of mothers pushing their babies along in hi-tech prams. A forlorn pink dummy has been dropped by the side of the path—I take a photo of it, though I'm not sure why. The usual stab of envy is absent today. Is it because I'll soon be leaving here, heading off towards the horizon? Or is the past finally receding? Whichever, it feels like progress.

By the time I return from my walk there's news—it's a baby boy, and both mother and infant are well. There's a flurry of family phone calls, and a glass of champagne to toast the new arrival.

Then I say my farewells, climb back into the van and drive away from the lucky grandparents.

insignificance

I'M STAYING ALONE on the Sunshine Coast in a unit belonging to an old schoolfriend. My friend is a mother of three, stepmother of another three, and a high-level public servant. Her life is full to bursting with human responsibilities. She longs for solitude, she tells me, and escapes to this light-filled unit when she needs to get away from all the people who need her. Our lives are mirror opposites.

The unit has a balcony overlooking the Pumicestone Passage, a narrow body of water between the mainland and the northern tip of Bribie Island. Every morning I sit on the balcony in the golden sunshine, sipping strong coffee and watching the pelicans float past. When I saw the film *Stormboy* as a child, I was fascinated by the friendship between the boy and his pet pelican, Mr Percival. I remember the horror of discovering that Mr Percival's mother had been shot dead by hunters. Even worse—the boy's mother and sister had both died suddenly in a car accident. The two motherless children, boy and bird, clinging to each other on a wide, wild beach.

I do an image search. I find scores of mother pelicans feeding their young, depicted in stained glass, carved wood, embroidery, tattoos, stone statues, over and over again. The winged mother and her hungry chicks. 'Pelicans are a symbol of empathy, nobility and goodness,' one website tells me. What, because they feed their young? Isn't that just natural and necessary?

'The symbolic depiction of a mother pelican feeding the little ones denotes a legend that originated prior to Christianity. According to the legend, the mother pelican, to save her babies from starving, wounded herself with her beak to feed them her blood.' The children were saved but the mother bled to death.

I wonder if I would have given my life for my child.

I hire a kayak and set off across Pumicestone Passage towards the island. The vessel pitches and rolls in the morning wind and I roll with it, enjoying the challenge of staying upright. When I was a child my mother gave me Arthur Ransome's book *Swallows and Amazons*, the sailing adventures of two gangs of kids in the Lake District of England, and their mock-war against grumpy Uncle Jim. I suspect Uncle Jim did not have children of his own; I recall that he was a memoirist. Back then my allegiances were with the children, of course, but these days I'd probably be on Uncle Jim's side.

I visited the Lakes in my early twenties, hiking the Cumbrian fells alone in the drizzle, imagining William Wordsworth hiking the same trails a century and a half before me. I'd never noticed how many different shades of grey there were in a watery sky, how many silvers rippled across the surface of a lake. The names on my map were like miniature poems—Crinkle Crag, Old Man of Coniston, Seat Sandal, Gummers How, Top o' Selside. I'd been backpacking solo for months, stalked by loneliness, but in that wild green landscape a kind of ecstasy had overtaken me. Alone in a place bereft of other humans, I was insubstantial, devoid of attachment, and free.

Today, paddling across the passage in the mid-winter sunshine, I feel the same quiet joy. Today I am happy in my solitude. It feels miraculous.

disturbance

I'M TRAVELLING SOUTH, free-camping in the bush. Each night I pull over somewhere quiet and secluded, lock the van doors and sleep soundly. Each morning I wake to the glorious sounds of the dawn chorus. After a few nights I feel like a hot shower, so I book into a caravan park. Around two in the morning I'm woken by a noise outside the van, which turns out to be my esky being stolen by three young men on bicycles. I see them lurking near the men's toilets so I wait until they've cycled off into the night, then walk down to the toilet block. A quick squat-check reveals they've left my esky perched on a toilet seat inside a locked cubicle. I don't fancy crawling under the door, so I head back to the van and go to sleep.

The next morning I visit the admin office and explain the situation to the manager. His face turns first white, then red.

'Are you telling me you're camping here all by yourself?' He launches into an expletive-laden lecture about how foolish and dangerous it is for women to travel alone without their families, and how we're just 'asking for trouble'.

I could point out to him that I'd been camping alone in the bush perfectly safely until I handed over money to stay in *his* caravan park—and anyway not all women have families.

But why waste my breath? With the esky restored to me, I pack up the van, drive out the gate and back to the bush. I've never been lectured by the dawn chorus.

~

Lying in the back of the van one night, I'm scrolling through social media feeds. In the middle of a series of images of adorable groodles and hilarious lolcats, there's a tweet announcing that 'a third of all species extinctions in the last hundred years have occurred in Australia'. The lesser bilby. The desert bandicoot. The dusky flying fox. The broad-faced potoroo. The big-eared hopping mouse. Gone. And then there are the birds and reptiles, the frogs and snails. All gone.

We love individual animals, we cry over caged animals, we spend whatever it takes to keep our pets alive. But we care so little about entire species that we allow them to become extinct. Maybe we can only love animals one at a time.

~

In a crowded café in a coastal tourist town there's one seat left, at a table where a tall dark-haired woman is sitting alone. I smile and ask, 'Do you mind if I join you?'

'Sure, that's fine,' she replies, unsmiling. She looks a bit younger than me and has a faint accent. I order breakfast and we begin talking. She's Dutch, she turned forty last week, and she's been travelling alone for the past five months through Asia and Australia. She has camped in the Snowy Mountains and at Wilsons Promontory, where kookaburras and wombats tried to take her food. She's recently been snorkelling on the Great Barrier Reef. Then she asks about me. Single, freelancer, traveller.

'Children?' she asks.

'No.'

At last she smiles, and it's a conspiratorial one. 'Me too. It's great, isn't it?'

There's a pause, and as I lean back slowly in my chair, her smile disappears. 'Ah, I should be more careful,' she says quietly.

I tell her how long I spent trying, and that I'm 'making the best of the situation'. I talk about my winter travels and describe the little campervan my stepfather made for me, rhapsodising about his ability to fix anything mechanical. I tell her he has a pacemaker and that, when he goes to hospital to get it checked, he declares he's off to 'tune up the rectifier in the engine room'. I'm trying to make her smile again, because we have more in common than not.

Walking to the beach one day I pass an elderly woman with a small child. The woman and I smile and nod at each other. A few metres down the road I turn and look back at them. They've stopped on the grassy verge to observe a blue-faced honeyeater feeding on palm fruit. As I watch them the child reaches out his hand to hold hers, and I am gut-punched with envy.

remembrance

I USED TO CALL Jay my *de facto stepgrandson*, always with a smile and an eye-roll to acknowledge the awkwardness of the phrase. Later, he became my *former de facto stepgrandson*.

On social media people have been complaining about the inadequacies of English when it comes to describing complicated family relationships.

What do I call my half-sister's uncle's partner's son from a previous relationship?

What do you call the woman your father was married to before he married your mother? I've no idea.

Our clan has to use all of these—'the wife of my ex-husband'—'the son of my ex-husband'—'the sister of my stepbrother'. It's exhausting.

Try filling out official forms and trying to explain that you have a 'partly-dependent-ex-stepdaughter-but-not-adopted-from-a-marriage-that's-now-in-trial-separation'.

After the break-up, Jay's maternal grandmother suggested we have a ceremony to formalise my relationship with him, but no one could figure out what I should be called. For Jay, it was simple. I was Sian.

—

I'm browsing in a Sydney bookshop. There's a small pink hardback in the middle of the bargains table, entitled *The little book of MOTHERHOOD*. I pick it up and flick through the pages. The page entries are short, the tone veers wildly from irony to sentimentality to dull facts.

> *Motherhood: because privacy is over-rated.*

> *No language can express the power and beauty and heroism and majesty of a mother's love.*

> *Every second, 4.3 babies are born.*

Would 0.3 percent of a baby look like one of my miscarried embryos? I'm about to put the book back on the bargains pile when I read this one:

> *Babies acquire their mother's experiences, learning fear at a young age from the odour their mums produce when they are in fight-or-flight mode.*

What did maternal terror smell like on the day my father drowned? A cocktail of sunscreen and sweat? These are my odours now, as I make my pilgrimage to beaches up and down the coast. I am not afraid when I'm beside the ocean, in the ocean, under the ocean; I don't know why. Or why I keep going back again and again to those thrashing breakers.

transference

I'VE DRIVEN THE VAN to the Murray River to attend a writers' festival in Mildura. One of the guest speakers is an American poet who recently lost his wife of four decades. It's an odd word, *lost*. A word that shrinks and expands depending on what it is that's lost. Lost like a backpacker in a rainforest? Lost like an embryo that won't stick? Lost like hope? The poet has written a collection of poems for his dead wife. Perhaps he would understand why I'm telling this story.

I discover an interview online with the poet. He tells the interviewer: 'The great danger of grief is that it overflows and takes you with it—there is a constant need to hold together—the writing form helps.' He talks about the difference between *knowing* and *understanding*. Poetry is concerned with knowing, he says, while scholarship is about understanding.

Poems are ways of conveying an experience of the world. A sort of transference. *Understanding* is more analytical, he says, a way of placing experience in context and coming to terms with it cognitively.

Do I write to *know* why I am childless? To *know* what I have done with my childlessness, and why? Or to *understand* those things? I want to do both. Maybe understanding can protect me from the pain of knowing.

But I want *you* to understand, too, so you don't jump to conclusions about people like me.

And what do I mean when I say *people like me* anyway? People who've lost something they cared about? We are legion. Likewise people who are lost and are trying to find themselves. Knowing and understanding are both useful, but surely it is *doing* that counts—what you *do* with all that knowing, all that understanding.

There are things I want *you* to do—those of you who have children. I want you to care for the ones you have not yet lost. Keep them safe, in their bodies and minds. Believe them when they tell you there is a crocodile under the bed, and if there is, banish it. I want you to care for the world they will occupy after they have lost you.

Care: another strange word. A word that shrinks and expands depending on what you care *about*. I don't care for oysters. Take care crossing the road. Care for this spinning blue planet so that the world—*their* world—is not lost.

～

My nephew sends me a chatty email. He's found an interesting new word he thinks I might like—*quodlibet*. It sounds like some kind of endangered mammal, but the dictionary tells me it's *a musical composition that combines several different melodies—usually popular tunes—in counterpoint, and often in a light-hearted, humorous manner. Example: 'Always Look on the Bright Side of Life' + 'I Like the Flowers, I Like the Daffodils' + 'Blue Moon'.*

I hum them one after the other, but it's not the same as hearing them at the same time. The counterpoint is missing, the sound of the notes meeting and harmonising to create a new piece of music.

Memoirs have the same limitations. If you recount your memories one at a time, in chronological order, you can't see the big picture. You miss out on the ways those stories echo and intersect, inflected with hindsight and insight, creating something like wisdom.

consequence

I'VE BEEN MISSING feeling astonished, missing the vicarious experience of astonishment, seeing the world through Jay's eyes. The older you get, the less often you're surprised—by anything. The shock of the new recedes and instead you see patterns and repetitions in every experience. Music sounds like other music you've heard. Faces look like other faces you've studied. Sea views are less breathtaking if you spend a lot of time by the sea.

But wonder hasn't entirely abandoned me. It's winter in the southern hemisphere, summer in the north, and I'm in Iceland, doing a walking trip with an old friend. We have spent a week driving and hiking through landscapes that look like a series of *Dr Who* planets.

We've climbed shale-littered volcanic mountains, ginger-ly skirting holes that spew boiling mud at unpredictable intervals. We've bathed in thermally heated rivers, lolling like pampered sprites in the warm water. We've driven through vast fields of congealed lava that look like the bilious vomit of a giant. We've crept out onto a high rocky ledge and watched as mammoth ice blocks crumble from a glacier's edge and float downriver to the sea. Every day we've found new sources of astonishment in the landscape.

Being perpetually astonished gives you a natural high (unless it's the perpetual daylight that's producing this joy; a pale blue sky at midnight is one of the most extraordinary things I've ever seen) that can lead to a state of mind where you start to believe you are the cause of every good thing that happens.

'The weather will be fine for whale watching tonight,' my friend predicts on a rainy day. It is.

'We're going to see puffins from the tour boat,' I promise her. We do.

'Björk will walk past us in Reykjavik,' I announce. On our first night back in town the Icelandic pop star duly strolls past us, sporting an orange leopard-print jumpsuit, and we're almost convinced we have caused her appearance.

But under this euphoric layer of magical thinking there's a darker substratum. In a land of ice and snow, rising temperatures can have dramatic consequences. Those giant ice blocks we saw floating down to the sea are the rubble from Iceland's disappearing glaciers, which, we learn, have lost about four billion tonnes of ice over the past century, half of it in the last twenty-five years. One of them has retreated more than five kilometres. Melting glaciers might make the land mass rise, which could lead to more volcanic eruptions here. But the melting of the polar ice caps could see ocean levels rise, too. The future for this little island is full of uncertainty.

I'm trying to tell myself it doesn't matter. I'll be long gone. But the future tugs on me like a child's hand, reminding me that I'm attached to this planet, these people, even the ones I'll never meet. Reminding me what's at stake.

—

It's autumn and I'm at home in Melbourne. The hot breeze coming through my bedroom window at midnight smells of eucalyptus smoke. Fires are burning in the east and the west and over the border to the north. It hasn't rained for a month and a half—no more than a smattering, anyway. The parks round here are a sickly yellow and scored with dark gashes where the earth has split like parched lips. I'm lying in the dark, talking to invisible children.

This drought, these fires, this heat, they're probably our fault.

The viral videos of plastic waste slicks a kilometre wide and twice as long, bobbing on the ocean's surface, crumbling into the ocean's depths, sneaking into the digestive systems of fish and sharks and dolphins and whales.

This, too, is our fault.

I'll probably be gone before these fires, these plastics, these poisoned fish make human life unbearable—at least in my country. I've lived more than half my life now.

It won't be my problem. It will be yours. I'm sorry.

Tonight I feel relief that I'll leave no genetic trace. I've condemned no child of mine to the clean-up job my generation is leaving for the next, and the one after that.

Perhaps my childlessness was an evolutionary inevitability. Something was faulty in me, and there was no point in reproducing any of it. But other people have been producing children, so here you all are, and now you will have to deal with the crap we're leaving behind.

I tell myself I don't have to care about you. I haven't smelled your hair after a shampoo bath. I haven't read you a bedtime story. I don't know what foods you've pushed to the edge of your plate, saving them till last because they're your favourites.

Maybe if I'd known you I would have tried harder. Perhaps I gave up too soon.

alliance

I HAVE A NEW housemate. My friend Melinda has sold her home, put her stuff in storage and moved into my spare room. We don't know how long this arrangement will last, but we're both glad for the company. She plays dance music in the kitchen and prepares meals with ingredients I've never tasted before. I pour us glasses of wine and sometimes we knock them over, laughing too hard. Sometimes one of us will weep, and neither of us minds.

Melinda was married once, long ago, to a man who developed a mental illness. Early one morning he found himself on a Sydney surf beach with a knife in his hand, hearing voices. Someone called the police. A bunch of men in uniforms surrounded him and shot him dead. I can see it in my mind's eye, another dead man lying on the sand, the red-headed giant striding towards the shore muttering *fee fi fo fum*.

Like me, Melinda has no children. But I have a dog now, a creature so black you can't see her eyes, and Jazzy trots between my room and Melinda's, hoovering up our toast crumbs and submitting to our hugs. Melinda and I are in a book club together, eight women in our forties, fifties and sixties. The book clubbers rarely talk about books these days. We share true stories from our own lives, stories as complex and involving as any novel we've read. Everyone in our book club has lost someone or something precious.

experience

SOME MEMORIES drain away like an ebb tide across mud
flats. Other memories remain vivid, inflected by colour.
There's an orange memory: sunset, 1970, a bay beach, late
summer heat, no wind. Coarse sand between my toes.
Fried-chicken grease between my fingers. A laughing boy
in the water who, back then, embodied joy. Andy was six,
the same age as me. He had two brothers, and our families
shared barbecues and beach trips. Andy made me laugh.
He was a fast runner and a good reader, and we competed
in both those things. He smiled a lot and when he smiled,
pleasure spread through me like sherbet. In grade four Andy
moved to another school and we lost touch. His circles were
not my circles. He became an orange-infused memory until
one night, about a decade ago, I saw him again.

It was winter and I was on a tram. The floor was smeared

with a cocktail of coffee, Coke and rain. Everyone on that tram had had enough of the long, cold working day, and no one looked more debilitated than the man sitting opposite me. He was a picture of misery. I looked away then looked back again. The shape of the face, the colour of the eyes. Something familiar from a time when all faces were new and therefore unlike any others. A time when astonishment came regularly. Those faces can stick in your memory for decades.

I could have said hello. We could have reminisced about the beach picnics and the primary-school spelling bees. I could have asked about his brothers and whether he still loved reading. But I was too shy, and he seemed too sad. I looked away.

At his funeral recently, there were speeches about a funny, clever, childless guy who was good at sports, delivered by middle-aged men who looked like my memories of Andy's dad, except they were his brothers. The day after the funeral I went back to that bay beach. The sea was frothy and brown, the sky the colour of slate, and it was drizzling. The horizon seemed closer. Everything was so much smaller than I remembered. Nothing was the same, especially not me.

Now, I thought to myself, *now* I would say hello on that tram. But now it's too late.

⁓

There's a poem I love by Judith Wright called 'Turning Fifty', in which the poet, tasting her fifty years in a cup of morning coffee—'bitter, neutral, clean'—talks of the years that 'scar flesh and mind'.

By the second half of our lives, we're all bearing these scars. People we loved have let us down or let us go. People we respected have failed to live up to our unreasonable expectations. Death has begun stalking the perimeter of our circle of attachment, picking people off. We can't protect them, or ourselves. As I meander along in the van, the digital post delivers news from people within that precious circle of mine. Dying parents, newborn grandchildren. Dying marriages, newborn love affairs. Meanwhile the pelicans float serenely past on the great bodies of water that punctuate the Australian coastline, oblivious to our little dramas.

It's winter and I've been noodling slowly up the east coast again in the van. Today I have a clear destination. I'm making a pilgrimage to the northern New South Wales beach where my father drowned half a century ago. The map on my phone leads me to a long spit, the Tweed River on one side and the ocean on the other. Late in the afternoon I pull up in the carpark and climb out of the van, looking for a path through the low dunes. There's a sign covered in red text warning of 'conditions that are often dangerous'. Was there a warning sign here the day our family came to this beach, the afternoon those two young people swam out further than they should have? I grab my towel from the back of the van and trudge through the dry sand to the ocean. The beach is long and narrow, tapering off to the north at the far end of the spit, and cradled to the south by a rocky headland. Banks of white and grey clouds drift overhead, occasionally parting for a glimpse of pale blue. A kilometre offshore there's a tiny island, a grass-topped haven for sea birds. A fierce wind is blowing from the horizon, and there are messy white-tops as far as the eye can see. I drop my towel and walk slowly towards the water's edge. As always, there is the shock of feeling no shock as I enter the amniotic warmth of these northern waters. Accustomed to the fierce bite of southern seas, my skin is grateful. But a tow is tugging at my thighs, promising to drag me towards the headland if I get out of my depth. I brace myself against the incoming waves, trying to decide. *There's no rush, Sian. No ticking clock now.* Besides, there may be a red-headed giant out there. I retreat to my towel. Some risks are not worth taking.

I spend the night camped illegally in the beach carpark. From the outside, my van still looks more like a bland delivery vehicle than a blonde nomad's cubbyhouse-on-wheels. I've rarely been questioned by parking inspectors. I cook myself a pasta meal on the gas stove, clean my teeth like an obedient child, get into bed and lock the van doors.

A couple of hours later I'm woken by a low muttering outside. Instantly alert, I can hear two voices, both male. There's another sound, a wet slicing: knife through flesh. I can hardly breathe. Shuffling footsteps, up and down beside the van. I try not to move in case they hear me. Right at this moment no one in the world knows where I am. No one is holding me in their mind, keeping me safe. What am I doing here alone, 'asking for trouble'?

After about fifteen minutes I hear the opening and closing of car doors and then an engine starts. It idles for a while, then slowly moves off into the night. I take deep breaths, trying to slow my heart rate, daring myself to unlock the van. The only sound outside is the low shoosh of the breakers on the other side of the dunes. I poke my head out into a dim glow from a nearby light pole. I step outside and the smell of putrefaction hits me. A couple of metres from where I'm parked there's a metal bench flecked with tiny lights. Fish scales.

I've camped beside a gutting station. In a bin next to the bench, there's a pile of bones, the skeletons of creatures who, just an hour ago, were swimming like quicksilver under the white-tops.

All those fears, all through my life. Have they been needless all along?

I sleep late in the morning and wake to a low cloud cover, but the wind is gentler today. Picking up my towel, I head back to the beach. The sea is calmer, the breakers even and unhurried. I walk south along the shore towards the headland and climb a steep path to the top. A tidal current is pushing the waves up against the rocky cliff: great gushing plumes that leap towards the sky and fall back down into the boiling froth. I sit on the grass at a safe distance, watching for patterns in the crashing sets, but there are none. The ocean comes and goes of its own accord.

Soon two teenage girls walk past me and climb down the slippery boulders at the end of the headland. Bikinis, wetsuit tops and long hair that flips around in the breeze. They find a rocky ledge they like and begin taking selfies. Their favourites are the ones where a wave crashes onto the rocks behind them, narrowly missing them as they snap photo after smiling photo.

I'm transfixed. *Conditions that are often dangerous*—didn't they see the sign? There's no rhythm here, no predictability. At any moment a slightly bigger wave could smash against the cliff and knock them both into the sea. People can disappear, just like that.

As I watch them pose with the rapacious ocean, I'm wondering—would I jump in after them? Knowing the dangers, would I try to rescue two girls I've never met before?

My adrenalised body knows the answer. It's already figured out a route down the jagged boulders to the sea, already assessed the direction I'd need to swim to drag them away from the rocks. My leg muscles have already tensed in preparation. Of *course* I would try to help, just as my father did all those years ago. When there is clear and present danger, we humans know how to respond. It's the slow-creeping threats we fail to register. The invisible carbon dioxide molecules leaking skyward, the drip, drip, drip of melting glaciers, the tides inching ever-higher up beaches like this one.

The girls have had enough. They clamber up to safety and I'm off duty. I pick my way down to the beach and follow my own footsteps in the sand, back to my towel. The sun has come out and the grey ocean has turned green. I stride into the surf and this time there is no clutching tow, no hidden rip. There's no red-headed giant waiting out the back for me. Not today. I catch wave after wave, tasting my fifty years there in the sea. Clean, neutral, bittersweet.

acknowledgments and gratitude

For their loving care: Margot Prior Hansen, John Hansen, David Prior, Yoni Prior, John Cumming, Reuben Cumming and David Jones.

For those vital early writing sessions: Jennifer Hansen.

For their wise and sensitive feedback: Di Websdale-Morrissey, Melinda Dundas, Suzy Zail, Yannick Thoraval, Fiona Scott-Norman, Mel Cranenburgh, Clare Strahan, Kristina Olsson and Michael Krockenberger.

For their generous hospitality: Marianna Serghi, Nola Wilmot, Sally Nowlan, Merrill Findlay, Kate Jeffery, Caroline Lee, Janine Mangiviona and Mark Stokes.

For two crucial writing residencies: Donata Carrazza and Helen Healy at the Mildura Writers Festival, and members of the RMIT NonFictionLab, caretakers of the Butterfly House.

For her expertise: Dr Sianan Healy.

For teaching me so much about writing: my RMIT colleagues and students and all the other writers I have taught and mentored.

For allowing me to quote from her wonderful book: Beth Spencer.

For permission to quote from Judith Wright's poem 'Turning Fifty': HarperCollins Publishers Australia.

For tracking down my celluloid father: National Film and Sound Archive of Australia.

For believing in this book: my agent Jenny Darling.

For all round support and brilliance: my editor Mandy Brett.

For the perfect cover: W. H. Chong.

publication acknowledgments

Earlier versions of several chapters of this book were first published in:

Sydney Morning Herald

Age

Sunday Age

Big Issue

O&G magazine

Grieve Anthology

'Changing Tracks', ABC Melbourne *Drive* program